LEARN TO SPEAK DUTCH
(WITHOUT EVEN TRYING)

Stephen Hernandez

Copyright © 2020 by Stephen Hernandez

All rights reserved. No part of this publication may be reproduced, distributed or transmitted in any form or by any means, without prior written permission.

www.stephenhernandez.co.uk

Publisher's Note: This is a work of non-fiction. Locales and public names are sometimes used for atmospheric purposes. Any resemblance to actual people, living or dead, or to businesses, companies, events, institutions, or locales is completely coincidental unless otherwise stated.

Book Layout © 2017 BookDesignTemplates.com

Learn to speak Dutch (without even trying) Stephen Hernandez. - 1st ed.

ISBN: 9798664849738

To all my subscribers at:

https://stephenhernandez.co.uk/

A new language is a new life.

—PERSIAN PROVERB

CONTENTS

Introduction to learning Dutch	P.7
1. Learning at home	P16
2. Learning Dutch on your own	P37
3. Practicing Dutch on your own	P39
4. A guide for the complete beginner	P50
5. Fluency	P55
6. Forgetting	P57
7. Dutch grammar	P83
8. Motivation	P92
9. Best Dutch TV shows	P100
10. Navigating the restaurant	P120
11. Partying	P128
12. Travel	P149
13. Learning like a child	P166
14. Speaking Dutch	P170
15. Learning without trying	P208
Conclusion	P219
Bibliography & online resources	P220

INTRODUCTION

LEARNING DUTCH

The purpose of this book is to teach you *how* to learn, rather than what to learn. It would be impossible to discuss the Dutch language's complete grammatical structure and, every Dutch word and its correct pronunciation in one book and if ever such a book were written it would be incredibly tedious. The aim of this book is to get you speaking Dutch to the extent you can hold a reasonable conversation with a native speaker and you can read and understand a newspaper and magazine article written in Dutch. Once you have progressed that far you will not need the help of any book, course, or teacher—you will just need to practice.

Make no mistake—learning a language when you are not living in a country where it is spoken is very difficult. Not only do you not have situations where you can practice your new found learning but you are constantly bombarded by your native language as soon as you leave the classroom or your chosen place of learning. In many ways it becomes a case of perseverance. I liken it to the starting of a new exercise regime. You enroll in a local gym (giving you the added incentive that you are actually paying to get fitter). At first you are full of enthusiasm and energy so you set yourself unrealistic goals. Instead of starting off walking and progressing to running, you start off at a mad sprint and quickly tire. The novelty soon wears off and going to the gym becomes an irksome duty. Then excuses for not going begin to kick in, and before you know it you have given up altogether.

- Absolutely anyone can learn Dutch.
- I'm completely serious.

It doesn't matter what your excuse is. Maybe you think you stink at languages. Maybe you think you're too lazy. Maybe you flunked out of high school Dutch (if it exists!) or maybe you just can't pronounce the word zwart (black) no matter how hard you try.

If you really want to learn Dutch, **you can do it.** Best of all you can do it without even trying. The only effort you have to make is to read this book (and even then you can skip the bits you don't like), make a concrete plan to study (one you can stick to), keep it fun (extremely important), and stay motivated over the long haul (self-explanatory).

- Decide on a simple, attainable goal to start with so that you don't feel overwhelmed.
- Make learning Dutch a lifestyle change.
- Invite Dutch into your daily life. That way, your brain will consider it something useful and worth caring about.

- Let technology help you out. The internet is absolutely great for learning Dutch—use it.
- Think about learning Dutch as a gateway to new experiences. Think of the fun things you want to do and turn them into language-learning opportunities.
- Make new friends. Interacting in Dutch is key—it will teach you to intuitively express your thoughts, instead of mentally translating each sentence before you say it. If you are a bit shy about getting the ball rolling with native speakers nearby, you can do this online (there is a whole chapter on this).
- Most of all do not worry about making mistakes. One of the most common barriers to conversing in a new language is the fear of making mistakes. But native speakers are like doting parents: any attempt from you to communicate in their language is objective proof that you are some sort of gifted genius. They'll appreciate your effort and even help you. The more you speak, the closer you'll get to the elusive ideal of "native fluency."

To start off with don't set yourself unrealistic goals or a grandiose study plan. Keep it simple. Set aside a small amount of time that you can reasonably spare even if it just means getting up 15 minutes earlier in the morning. If you set that time aside and avoid distractions that 15 minutes will be invaluable. Above all make it as fun as possible. No one said learning a new language was easy but neither should it be irksome.

You can use this book in tandem with any other learning resource you may be using at the moment if that resource is working for you. At some point, though, you will find you have your particular way of learning, and discovering that is very important. Once you find what works, you will have achieved an important milestone, and your learning will accelerate accordingly.

I hope that with this book you will find your "way" sooner rather than later. That is what I designed it to do.

This book has no strict order (you can jump to and from chapters if you want), no particular rules to follow, and I definitely do not take anything for granted except the fact that you want to learn to speak Dutch and most probably want the experience to be as painless as possible.

I want to make it clear once again (as it is important), that this book is not designed to "teach" you Dutch. It is designed to help you learn how to teach yourself to speak Dutch with the least effort possible—hence, the sub-title: "without even trying". It gives you a process and pointers on how to learn Dutch effectively and easily. Consider it an autodidactic guide.

It is also a guide to learning subconsciously. By subconsciously, I do not mean that you go to sleep listening to tapes in Dutch or practice some kind of self-hypnosis. What we are aiming at is picking up Dutch without forcing the issue. The greatest aim in learning any language is being able to think in that language and not be aware that you are doing it. Then, you speak automatically without over thinking the process. Stick with me and you will obtain that goal.

Sound impossible? It won't be by the time you have finished this book.

A journey of a thousand miles begins with a single step.

Yeah, we've all heard that one from a thousand language teachers.

As far as advice goes, that saying is about as useful as an ashtray on a motorbike.

Think about it. If you're stranded in a foreign wilderness with no idea about *how* to get where you want to go, you'll have an extraordinarily difficult time getting there no matter how many footsteps you take. In fact, you'll probably end up going around in circles.

But if you've got a map and compass, as well as some decent navigating skills, you're likely to be on your way a lot faster.

In the same way, when you're starting to learn a new language, it helps to have a road map to both guide you along and guarantee that you're still headed in the right direction when you get stuck or feel lost.

Just like physical maps, a map for language learning should be based on what other people have seen. There are a number of polyglots and dedicated language learners out there who have become cartographers of the linguistic frontier. We will be drawing on their collective experience.

We will take this collective language learning experience, along with some scientific and technical know-how, and set out on the path to learning a new language in double time.

Here are some basic strategies to get you started:

- Become your own coach—develop goals and strategies. If you have heard of bullet journals, now is a good time to put one into practice. If this fails to ring the smallest of bells in the lockers of your memory, Google it and decide if you like the idea—it comes in very handy when learning a new language.
- A lot of the time, when we start something new, we make vague statements like, "I want to be able to speak well as quickly as possible," or, "I'm going to study Dutch as much as I possibly can." This can be a problem because, when we create such vague goals, it can be very difficult to achieve any sort of meaningful result. That's why orienting your Dutch learning odyssey should start with the use of two techniques: **SMART goals** and **metacognitive strategies**.
- **SMART,** in this case, is an acronym that means **S**pecific, **M**easurable, **A**chievable, **R**esults, **T**ime-

bound. The synopsis of this is that you need to make really, really concrete goals that can be achieved (even if you're incredibly lazy—see next chapter). Setting realistic goals like this is an essential skill for anyone studying by themselves, as well as anyone who wishes to maximize their study time.

- **Metacognitive strategies** involves three steps. First, you plan. Ask yourself what your specific goals are and what strategies you're going to use to achieve them. Second, start learning and keep track of how well you do every day. Are you having problems that need new solutions? Write that down. Are you consistently succeeding or failing in a certain area? Keep track of that, too. And the third and final step, after a few weeks to a month, it is time to **evaluate yourself**. Were you able to achieve your goals? If not, why? What strategies did and didn't work? Then the whole process repeats again.

These two techniques naturally fit together quite well, and they're both indispensable for making sure you're cooking with gas every time you sit or lie down to study.

Total immersion (i.e., living in a Dutch-speaking country) and speaking, seeing, hearing, reading and writing it all the time is, of course, the ultimate way to learn and is certainly the ultimate goal to strive for. Most of us aren't free to move from country to country as we please and must make decisions about when the best time would be for us to go to that oh-so-wonderful country we've been daydreaming about for countless hours. So, this book is aimed mainly at people who are studying from home in their native country but also has a large travel section for before you travel.

Enjoy yourself.

Languages can be difficult to master. Even the easiest of languages for English speakers can take six hundred hours to conquer, according to the Foreign Service Institute, and perhaps much more than that if you want to do something with it professionally. This is not something you can do day in, day out without getting some pleasure out of the whole *ordeal.*

Thankfully, language is as human an obstacle as it gets and is naturally tied to amazing and fulfilling rewards. Think about how wonderful it is or could be to read your favorite Dutch author in the original, or understand a Dutch film without having to look at the sub-titles, or most amazing of all, hold a conversation with someone in their native language! Language is the thing that connects us to other people and the social benefits are extremely powerful.

Just think about how often you check Facebook. Why are social networking sites so popular? Because any information connected to other people is inherently seductive. So, from the get-go, make sure that you use your language skills for what they were made for—socializing.

Sometimes, when your schedule is crazy, you'll be tempted to jettison the "fun" things that made you attracted to learning Dutch in the first place to get some regular practice in. Maybe you'll skip your favorite Dutch TV show because you can't understand it without subtitles yet (more on this later), or you'll forget to keep up with the latest news on your favorite Dutch singer or band.

Make time for the things that got you started. They're what motivate you and push you through when language learning seems like a brutal punishment.

Really, it's all about balance. The steps are all here, laid out for you.

Only by starting out on the journey will you gain intuitive control, the sense of masterful dexterity like that of a professional athlete or a samurai warrior.

You have your map.

Now you just need to take those first steps ...

CHAPTER ONE

LEARNING AT HOME
(even if you're really lazy)

Do you have hopes and dreams of speaking a language fluently, but you're too lazy to study?

So do many people, but they give up before they've even started because it just seems like so much effort towards an intangible goal. And seriously—who *wants* to study?

But what if I told you that your laziness, far from being a limitation, could actually make you great at learning Dutch?

Read on (if you can be bothered) to find out why the lazy way is often the best way and learn ways you can leverage your laziness to learn a language effectively at home.

Lazy people find better ways to do things

If you were a builder at the end of the 19th century, life was hard. Long hours. Bad pay. Little regard for health and safety. If you were really unlucky, it could even cost you your life: five men died during the construction of the Empire State Building, and 27 died working on the Brooklyn Bridge.

Mortality rates amongst builders in Victorian Britain were even more horrendous. In short, being a builder was a dangerous job.

What qualities did builders need in such a demanding and dangerous job?

Tenacity? Diligence? Stamina?

No. Not at all.

In 1868, a young construction worker named Frank Gilbreth, while observing colleagues to understand why some bricklayers were more effective than others, made a startling discovery.

The best builders weren't those who tried the hardest. The men Gilbreth learned the most from were the laziest ones.

Laying bricks requires repeating the same skilled movements over and over again: the fewer motions, the better. In an attempt to conserve energy, the "lazy" builders had found ways to lay bricks with a minimum number of motions. In short, they'd found more effective ways to get the job done.

But what do lazy bricklayers have to do with learning Dutch, apart from the fact that I worked as one for a while? (I wasn't very good at laying bricks, but I was excellent at being lazy!)

Well, inspired by his lazy colleagues, Gilbreth went on to pioneer "time and motion study," a technique that streamlines work systems and is still used today in many fields to increase productivity. You know that person in the operating room who passes scalpels to the surgeon and wipes their brow? Gilbreth came up with that idea.

Hiring someone to pass you things from 20 centimeters away and wipe the sweat off your own forehead? It doesn't get much lazier than that. Yet it helps surgeons work more efficiently and probably saves lives in the process.

The bottom line? The lazy way is usually the smartest way.

Over the years, Gilbreth's ideas have been attributed to people like Bill Gates, who is (falsely) reported to have said: "I will always choose a lazy person to do a difficult job because he will find an easy way to do it." (This attribution, although factually incorrect, makes a nice motivational poster to hang in your office.)

The lazy way

One of the most embarrassing episodes in my life (and there are quite a few, believe me!) was when I unadvisedly went to a parents' evening at my young daughter's primary school. The teacher asked each child in turn what their fathers did for a living. My daughter's response: "He lies on the sofa with his hands down his trousers."

Actually, that is partly true, although you may be relieved to know that I don't spend *all* my time with my hands down my trousers. If there's one thing I love more than writing, listening to the radio, and browsing the web, it's sitting or lying on the sofa in my pants, reading or watching TV—a lot of the time in Dutch. Fortunately, with regards to writing this book, these activities aren't mutually exclusive, so I'm always on the lookout for ways to combine my favorite pastimes.

I've scoured the web to find the best resources to learn Dutch, and this book contains my findings. Hopefully, the information contained herein will save you a lot of time and money spent on useless systems and pointless exercises and will repay your faith in me. When you speak Dutch (which you will), please remember to recommend it to your friends. Even if you don't use a computer, there is enough basic information here to get you started on your path to learning Dutch. But I would strongly advise getting on the internet if you intend to learn from home with some degree of success.

If your school was anything like mine, you may have some experience learning languages with the "try harder" approach: page after page of grammar exercises, long vocabulary lists, listening exercises about stationary or some other excruciatingly boring topic. And if you still can't speak the language after all that effort? Well, you should try harder.

But what if there's a better way to learn a language? A lazier way, that you can use to learn a language at home and, with less effort?

A way to learn by doing things you actually enjoy? A way to learn by having a laugh with native speakers? A way to learn without taking your pajamas off?

There is.

Don't get me wrong. Languages take time and effort; there's no getting around that. This isn't about being idle.

It's about finding effective ways to learn (remember: SMART and metacognitive strategies?) so you can stop wasting time and energy on stuff that doesn't work. With that in mind, I've put together a collection of lazy (but highly effective) ways to learn a language at home or away.

They'll help you:

- Speak a language better by studying less!
- Go against "traditional" language learning methods to get better results.
- Get fluent in a language while sitting around in your undies and drinking beer (this isn't compulsory).

Don't study (much).

A lot of people try to learn a language by "studying." They try really hard to memorize grammar rules and vocabulary in the hope that one day, all the pieces will come together and they'll magically start speaking the language.

Sorry, but languages don't work that way.
Trying to speak a language by doing grammar exercises is like trying to make bread by reading cookbooks. Sure, you'll pick up some tips, but you'll never learn how to bake unless you're willing to get your hands dirty.

Languages are a learn-by-doing kind of a deal. The best way to learn to speak, understand, read, and write a language is by practicing speaking, listening, reading, and writing. That doesn't mean you should never study grammar or vocabulary. It helps to get an idea of how the language works. But if you dedicate a disproportionate amount of time to that stuff, it'll clutter your learning experience and hold you back from actually speaking Dutch.

You'll learn much faster by *using the language.*

Now, if you're totally new to language learning, you may be wondering how you can start using a language you don't know yet. If you're learning completely from scratch, a good textbook can help you pick up the basics. But avoid ones that teach lots of grammar rules without showing you how to use them in real life. The best textbooks are the ones that give you lots of example conversations and introduce grammar in bite-size pieces.

As soon as you can, aim to get lots of exposure to the Dutch language being used in a real way. If you're a lower-level learner, you can start by reading books that have been simplified for your level (called graded readers). Look for ones accompanied by audio so you can work on your listening at the same time.

If you can, keep a diary or journal of your experience with different methods of learning. Bullet journals are great for this. Never heard of them? They are basically a sort of a cross between a diary and a to-do list. Keeping one will help you see what works for you and what doesn't, and also to chart your progress. You can buy readymade ones to suit you or design your own. You can use it for motivation when you feel like you are getting nowhere, as you will see at a glance all the progress you have made. Believe me, you will be surprised at how far you have come and sometimes you just need a little reminder to give you that motivational push. You will also be able to see what areas you need to improve in and the types of things you are best at. When you are feeling low, go back to the stuff you are best at.

Consider how a child has learned to speak a language. Presumably, unless it was a precocious genius, it did not start off by reading a primer in grammar. Children start off by observing and identifying. Naming and pronunciation comes from hearing the description of the object from others, usually adults, or other kids fluent in the language.

This is something you can do right now, right this minute. Start off by naming in Dutch the objects that surround you, write the Dutch name for the object on a Post-it Note, and stick it on the object. You can find the Dutch translation for any household object online or in a two-way dictionary. I would advise using an online dictionary if you can, as these usually include a guide to pronunciation that you can actually listen to without trying to do it phonetically.

Put the Post-it Note at eye level or some place you will encounter it immediately upon looking at the object. Begin by saying the objects name out loud—,or perhaps, if you have company, in your head. At this point, don't worry too much if your friends and family think you have gone a little crazy. You are learning a new language; they are not. Give yourself a pat on the back instead.

Below is a short list of some common things around the house to give you a start and the idea behind this method. Remember to write the name of the object in **Dutch** only. Preferably, put your Post-it Note on an immovable object (your spouse or significant other might take exception to having a Post-it Note stuck on their forehead, and so might your dog or cat).

- Put the Post it Notes on everything in your house (use a two-way dictionary). It is a great way to learn nouns (the name of things). Don't forget to put if they are feminine, masculine or neuter (they are in brackets) and we will be touching on them later. Soon you will begin to identify these objects in Dutch without consciously thinking about it.

(de) woning	the house
(de) deur	the door
(het) raam	the window
(de) stoel	the chair
(de) kruk	the stool
(de) lamp	the lamp
(de) televisie	the television
(de) kast	the closet
(de) wc	the toilet
(de) keuken	the kitchen
(het) fornuis	the cooker
(de) koelkast	the fridge

(de) kamer	the room
(de woonkamer)	the living room
(de bank)	the couch
(de) slaapkamer	the bedroom
(het bed)	the bed
(de) badkamer	the bathroom
(de) douche	the shower
(het) bad	the bath
(de) bijkeuken	the scullery
(de) garage	the garage
(de) tuin	the garden
(de) zolder	the attic
(de) kelder	the basement
(de) trap	the stairs
(de) deurbel	the doorbell
(de) kandelaar	the candle holder
(de) behang	the wall paper
(het) wandrek	the wall shelf
(de) gordijnroede	the curtain rod
(de) frituurpan	the fryer
(de) keukenrol	the paper towel
(de) servethouder	the napkin holder
(de) wasmand	the laundry basket
(het) wasmiddel	the laundry detergent
(het) blik	the dustpan
(de) glasreiniger	the squeegee
(de) stoffer	the duster
(de) prullenbak	the trashbin
(de) rubberen handschoenen	the rubber gloves
(de) lap	the rag

Dutch Articles

The short defining word before the noun is really part of the noun. It is called *an article*. You may not have learned this at school, but in English, there is only one definite article: *the*. That is because the word "the" points to a very specific thing. For example, you may tell someone, "I want the book," assuming that they will bring you the book you have in mind.

However, if you tell them, "I want a book," you will get whatever book they choose to hand you! That is because the words "a" or "an" or "some" are indefinite articles and point to a general group of items, things, people or places.

Articles can be definite (specific) or indefinite (general).

When it comes to definite articles, Dutch has an extra layer of complexity compared to English. In Dutch, there are two definite articles: *de* and *het*. Whether you use *de* or *het* depends also on the gender of the noun.

There are three genders in Dutch: masculine, feminine, and neuter. *De* is used with masculine and feminine nouns. *Het* is used with neuter nouns. Each noun has a gender and some nouns have two genders. Both, *de* and *het*, can be used with the nouns that are masculine and neuter.

There are a few rules that govern the articles of some of the nouns. You have to memorize the articles of the rest. First, let's go over the rules and then discuss how to memorize the articles of the nouns.

Plural nouns always take the article *de*, regardless of their gender.

Singular	Plural
De man	De mannen (the men)
Het kind	De kinderen (the children)
Het boek	De boeken (the books)
Het koekje	De koekjes (the cookies)

Singular diminutive nouns (verkleinwoorden) take the article *het*.

- Het koekje (the cookie)
- Het huisje (the little house)
- Het kindje (the little child)

Infinitives take the article *het*

- Het lopen (to walk)
- Het lezen (to read)
- Het spelen (to play)

Nouns that refer to persons take the article *de*

- De man (man)
- De vrouw (woman)
- De vriend (friend)

Nouns that end with -ing, -er, -held, -in, or -aar take the article *de*

- De vergadering (meeting)
- De bakker (baker)
- De overheid (government)
- De vriendin (girlfriend)
- De ambtenaar (civil servant)

Two syllable nouns that start with be-, ge-, ver-, or ont- take the article *het*

- Het beheer (management)
- Het geluid (sound)
- Het verband (connection, context, relation)
- Het onthaal (reception)

Trees, plants, vegetables, and fruits take the article *de*

- De eik (oak)
- De orchidee (orchid)
- De spinazie (spinach)
- De appel (apple)

Nouns that end with -isme, -ment, -sel, or -um take the article *het*

- Het activisme
- Het instrument
- Het voedsel (food)
- Het museum

Sports take the article *het*

- Het tennis
- Het voetbal (football)
- Het judo

Sit around in your undies (just like The Naked Trader!)
Next, you'll need to practice speaking. Luckily, you can now do this on Skype, so you only need to get dressed from the waist up.

The best place for online conversation classes is italki (italki.com) Here, you can book one-on-one conversation lessons with native speakers called community tutors.

Talking to native speakers

This is, by far, the best way to learn a foreign language, but there's one problem with this method that no one talks about.

To start with, those native speakers everyone is going on about may not want to talk to you.

When you start speaking a foreign language, it's all mind blanks, silly mistakes, and sounding like a two-year-old, which makes communication slow and awkward.

It's not you that's the problem. You have to go through that stage if you want to speak a foreign language.
But you need the right people to practice with. Supportive ones who encourage you to speak and don't make you feel embarrassed when you get stuck or make mistakes.

The best place to find these people?

The internet.

The fastest (and most enjoyable way) to learn a language is with regular, one-on-one speaking practice. Online tutors are perfect because it's so easy to work with them—you can do a lesson whenever it suits you and from wherever you have an internet connection, which makes it simple to stick to regular lessons.

Let's just run through how to sign up with italki, although the procedure is much the same with other online sites:
- Go to italki.com.
- Fill in your details, including which language you're learning.
- Once you get to the main italki screen, you'll see your profile with your upcoming lessons. At the moment, it says zero, so let's go ahead and set one up.
- Click on "find a teacher."
- Here, you'll find filters like "price," "availability," and "specialties." Set these to fit in with your budget, schedule, and learning goals.
- Explore the teacher profiles and watch the introduction videos to find a teacher you'll enjoy working with.
- Click on "book now," and you'll see their lesson offers.

Informal tutoring

When choosing your lessons, you'll often see "informal tutoring," which is a pure-conversation class. This kind of lesson is great value because the tutor doesn't have to prepare anything beforehand. They just join you on Skype and start chatting

Booking your first lesson

Once you've chosen the kind of lesson you'd like, choose the time that suits you, and voilà, you've just booked your first lesson with an online tutor! Well done—I know it can feel a little intimidating at first, but creating opportunities to practice is the most important thing you can do if you want to learn to speak Dutch. Remember: practice, practice, practice. Have I stressed that enough?

The difference between professional tutors and community tutors

When choosing a teacher, you'll also see a filter called "teacher type" and the option to choose between professional teachers and community tutors. What's the difference?

Professional teachers are qualified teachers vetted by italki—they have to upload their teaching certificate to gain this title. These classes tend to be more like "classic language lessons." The teacher will take you through a structured course, preparing lessons beforehand and teaching you new grammar and vocabulary during each lesson.

Good for:

- If you're a total beginner.
- You're not sure where to start, and you'd like guidance from an expert.

Community tutors are native speakers who offer informal tutoring, where the focus is 100% on conversation skills. They'll give you their undivided attention for an hour while you try to speak, and they'll help by giving you words and corrections you need to get your point across.

Good for:
- If you've already spent some time learning the theory and you feel like you're going round in circles. You need to put it into practice. (Remember!)
- You're happy to take control of your own learning by suggesting topics and activities you'd like to try.
- You're on a budget—these classes are usually very good value.

If both of these options are out of your budget range, you can also use italki to find a language partner, which is free—you find a native speaker of the language you're learning (in this case, Dutch, of course!) who also wants to learn your native language, and you teach each other. (You will find a lot of Dutch speakers who want and are very willing to practice their English, believe me. You can also use your social media connections, that's what it's there for—socializing! Haven't got any Dutch-speaking friends on Facebook? Make some.)

Important tip for finding the right tutor

Experiment with a few different tutors until you find one you click with. When you find a tutor you get along well with, they end up becoming like a friend—you'll look forward to meeting them and will be motivated to keep showing up to your lessons.

Prepare for your first lesson

Spending a little time preparing will allow you to focus during the lesson and get as much out of it as possible. These little gems of Dutch can also be used to open a conversation with a native Dutch speaker in any real-life situation, not just chatting online

Learn the basic pleasantries

"Hello," "goodbye," "please," "sorry," and "thank you" will take you a long way!

Learn basic communication phrases

It's important to try and speak in the language as much as possible without switching back into English. Those moments when you're scrambling for words and it feels like your brain's exploding—that's when you learn the most!

Here are some phrases to get you going (if you are not sure about pronunciation go to the chapter on travel:

Good Morning **Goedemorgen**

Good Day	**Goedemiddag**
Good Evening	**Goedenavond**
Good Night	**Goedenacht**
Hi / Bye	**Hoi / Hallo / Daag / Doei**
Goodbye	**Tot ziens**
See you later	**Tot straks**
See you soon	**Tot zo**
Please	**Alstublieft / Alsjeblieft**
Thank you	**Dank u wel / Dank je wel**
Thank you very much	**Hartelijk bedankt**
You're welcome	**Graag gedaan**
I'm sorry / Excuse me	**Sorry**
Pardon me	**Pardon**
Yes / No	**Ja / Nee**
How are you? (formal)	**Hoe gaat het met u?**
How are you? (informal)	**Hoe gaat het?**

Fine / Very well	**Goed / Heel goed**
So so / Bad	**Het gaat / Slecht**
I'm tired / sick	**Ik ben moe / ziek**
I'm hungry / thirsty	**Ik heb honger / dorst**
What's your name? (formal)	**Hoe heet u?**
What's your name? (informal)	**Hoe heet je?**
My name is (I'm called)...	**Ik heet...**
I am...	**Ik ben...**
Nice to meet you	**Aangenaam (kennis te maken)**
Mister / Misses / Miss	**meneer / mevrouw / mejuffrouw**
Where are you from? (formal)	**Waar komt u vandaan?**
Where are you from? (informal)	**Waar kom je vandaan?**
I am from the Netherlands	**Ik kom uit Nederland**
Where do you live? (formal)	**Waar woont u?**
Where do you live? (informal)	**Waar woon je?**
I live in America	**Ik woon in Amerika**

How old are you? (formal)	**Hoe oud bent u?**
How old are you? (informal)	**Hoe oud ben je?**
I am ____ years old	**Ik ben ... jaar (oud).**
Do you speak Dutch? (formal)	**Spreekt u Nederlands?**
Do you speak English? (informal)	**Spreek je Engels?**
I [don't] speak...	**Ik spreek [geen]...**
I don't speak ... very well	**Ik spreek niet zo goed...**
I [don't] understand	**Ik begrijp het [niet.]**
I [don't] know	**Ik weet het [niet.]**
How much is it?	**Wat kost het?**
I'd like...	**Ik wil graag...**
Cheers!	**Cheers!**
Have fun!	**Veel plezier!**
Good luck!	**Veel succes!**
Be careful!	**Wees voorzichtig!**
That is great / terrible!	**Dat is geweldig / vreselijk!**

I love you (informal)	**Ik hou van je**
I love you (all)	**Ik hou van jullie**
How funny / odd!	**Wat vreemd!**
What a pity!	**Wat jammer!**
What is this / that?	**Wat is dit / dat?**

CHAPER TWO

LEARNING DUTCH ON YOUR OWN

If you want to learn Dutch independently, you're going to need a few things in your head-locker.

- Motivation (to keep going)
- Focus/Mindfulness (to be effective)
- Time/Patience (for everything to sink in)

Without these three things, it's impossible to learn a language.

There seems to be one killer rule to set yourself up for success: **keep it simple!**

With tonnes of Dutch websites, apps, and courses out there, it can be tempting to jump from one to the next.

But there's one golden rule to remember ...

It's usually more effective to calmly work your way through one book or stick with one study method than to try different things out of curiosity. It is therefore doubly important to pick the right study methods. The best will

be referred to in this book so you don't waste your valuable study time.

The focus you'll get from this keeps self-doubt away and helps you learn more deeply.

If you are learning by yourself, for whatever reasons, you will have to *work* a little bit every day at your Dutch to succeed. Dedicating a regular amount of time every day, no matter how little, is more productive than learning sporadically in large chunks.

You will need to spend a lot of your time listening to Dutch. If you don't, how do you expect to ever be able to follow along in a conversation?

If you are completely new to studying and like to learn via your computer or mobile, then there is a pretty neat way of starting off your Dutch adventure online: https://www.learndutch.org/ it is a very easy way to start off your learning experience and will supply you with a lot of handy tips for your language learning in the future. Best of all it's free!

Self-study and online learning are the most flexible ways to learn anything as you can base your learning around your lifestyle rather than working to the schedule of a rigid language school. By being able to work on your Dutch in your lunch break, on your commute, in a cafe, or at home, you have the flexibility to learn at your own speed, making it much easier to be successful.

CHAPTER THREE

PRACTICING DUTCH ON YOUR OWN

It is very important to regularly practice the Dutch you have learned even if it is just talking out loud to yourself. To really succeed in Dutch (become fluent), it is essential to practice with a native speaker, but until you have found someone to practice with, here are some ways to practice by yourself.

Think in Dutch

One of the main things about learning to speak a language is that you always have to learn to think in the language.

If you're always thinking in English when you speak Dutch, you need to translate everything in your head while you speak. That's not easy and takes time.

It doesn't matter how fluent your Dutch is; it's always hard to switch between two languages in your mind.

That's why you need to start thinking in Dutch as well as speaking it. You can do this during your daily life.

If you discover a new word in Dutch, reach for your Dutch dictionary rather than your Dutch-to-English dictionary. (Don't have dictionaries?—Buy some. You will need them; they can be your best friends while learning Dutch.)

Think out loud

Now that you're already thinking in Dutch—why don't you think out loud?

Talking to yourself whenever you're on your own is a great way to improve your language-speaking skills.

When you're reading books in Dutch, try doing it out loud, too.

The problem with speaking on your own is when you make mistakes. There's nobody there to correct you.

However, it's helpful to improve your ability to speak out loud, even if you make the occasional error.

Talk to the mirror

Stand in front of a mirror and talk in Dutch.

You could pick a topic to talk about and time yourself.

Can you talk about soccer for two minutes? Can you explain what happened in the news today for three minutes?

While you're talking, you need to watch the movements of your mouth and body.

Don't allow yourself to stop. If you can't remember the particular word, then you need to express the same thing with different words.

After a couple of minutes, it's time to look up any words you didn't know. This will allow you to discover which words and topics you need to work to improve.

Fluency over grammar

The most important thing when speaking isn't grammar; **it's fluency**.

You don't want to be stopping and starting all the time. You need to be able to have free-flowing conversations with native speakers.

Don't allow yourself to stop and stumble over phrases. A minor error here and there doesn't matter.

You need to make yourself understood rather than focus on everything being perfect.

Try some Tongbrekers (tongue-twisters)

"Tongbrekers" is the Dutch word for tongue-twisters. This includes words or phrases that are difficult to say at speed. Tongue-twisters are not only good for impressing people, they can also be helpful. Dutch tongue-twisters are a great way to practice and improve pronunciation of difficult sounds and fluency. And these sentences are not only for children or students. Actors, politicians, and public speakers practice speaking with these difficult sentences.

Below are some of the most popular Dutch tongue-twisters. Try to say them as quickly as you can, and if you master them, you can impress your friends as a confident speaker.

There is an English translation under each Dutch tongue-twister, some information on the origin and tips on learning

1. Wij smachten naar achtentachtig prachtige nachten bij achtentachtig prachtige grachten.

Translation: We yearn for eighty-eight beautiful nights at eighty-eight beautiful canals.

Pretty easy in English, right?

The challenging element in this sentence is the ch / g sound which is in the back of your throat and is difficult to pronounce when you are learning Dutch.

2. Toen Koos Koos koos, koos Koos Koos terug.

Translation: When Koos (typical name for a Dutch man) chose Koos, Koos chose Koos back.

In this sentence the letter combination oo is important.

3. Zelden zagen wij zagende zagen zo zagen als wij onze zagende zagen zagen zagen.

Translation: (kind of difficult in English as well) Rarely did we see sawing saws so sawing as we saw our sawing saws.

The complication comes from the past tense of zien (zagen) and the plural noun for a saw (zagen)

4. Als een potvis op een pispot pist, heb je een pispot vol potvispis.

Translation: If a whale pisses in a chamber pot, then you have a chamber pot full of whale piss.

5. Liesje leerde Lotje lopen langs de lange lindelaan maar Lotje wou niet leren lopen dus liet Liesje Lotje staan.

Translation: Liesje taught Lotje to walk along the long lime tree avenue but Lotje didn't want to learn to walk, so Liesje let Lotje stand.

6. De knappe kapper kapt heel knap maar het knaapje van de knappe kapper kapt nog knapper dan de knappe kapper kappen kan.

Translation: The handsome hairdresser cuts very well but the helper of the handsome hairdresser cuts even better than the handsome hairdresser can cut.

7. Voordat was was was, was was kaarsvet.

Translation: Before wax was wax it was suet.

This tongue twister is an exercise with the w and the v.

If you can master tongue-twisters in Dutch, you'll find that you'll improve your overall ability to pronounce challenging words in Dutch.

Listen and repeat over and over

Check out Dutch-language TV shows or movies to improve your Dutch (there is a chapter dedicated to this later on).

Listen carefully and, then pause and repeat. You can attempt to replicate the accent of the person on the screen.

If you need some help to understand the meaning, turn on subtitles for extra help. If you come across a word you don't recognize, you can look it up in your Dutch dictionary.

Learn some Dutch songs

If you want a really fun way to learn a language, you can learn the lyrics to your favorite songs.

You can start with children's song and work yourself up to the classics.

And if you want a greater challenge, check out the Dutch rappers. If you can keep up the pace with some of these hip-hop artists, you're doing great!

Learn phrases and common sayings

Instead of concentrating on learning new words—why not try to learn phrases and common sayings?
You can boost your vocabulary and learn how to arrange the words in a sentence like a native speaker.

You need to look out for how native speakers express stuff. You can learn a lot from listening to others.

Imagine different scenarios

Sometimes, you can imagine different scenarios in which you have to talk about different kinds of things.

For example, you can pretend to be in an interview for a job in a Dutch-speaking country.

You can answer questions such as: "What are your biggest weaknesses?" and "Why do you want to work for us?"

When you have already prepared for such circumstances, you'll know what to say when the time comes.

Change the language on your devices

Consider changing your phone, computer, tablet, Facebook page, and anything else with a language option to Dutch. This is an easy way to practice Dutch since you'll see more of the vocabulary on a daily basis.

For example, every time you look at your phone, you'll see the date in Dutch, reinforcing the days of the week and months of the year. Facebook will ask you if you would like to "vriend toevoegen", teaching you the verb that means "to add."

Seeing a few of the same words over and over again will help the language feel more natural to you, and you'll find it becomes easier to incorporate them into everyday life with very little effort involved!

Research in Dutch

How many times a day do you Google something that you're curious about? If you use Wikipedia a few times a week, go for the Dutch version of the website first. Next time you need information about your favorite celebrity, look at their page in Dutch and see how much you can understand before switching the language to English!

Pick up a Dutch newspaper

You can read Dutch newspapers online. I recommend *De Telegraf* (The Telegraph), One of the most widely circulated

Dutch newspapers. The first edition was released in 1893 and published by Dutch media and publishing company "Telegraaf Media Groep". You can also download apps and read the news on your phone. You can read the articles out loud to practice Dutch pronunciation in addition to reading skills. This is also a great way to stay informed about what is happening in Dutch-speaking countries and helps if you get in a Dutch conversation.

Play games in Dutch
Once your phone is in Dutch, many of your games will appear in Dutch, too. Trivia games force you to be quick on your feet as you practice Dutch, as many of them are timed. If that isn't for you, WordBrain offers an interesting vocabulary challenge in Dutch! (See the chapter on apps).

Watch TV Shows and You Tube videos

Don't knock Dutch soap operas or dramas until you try them! If you follow any British soaps, you will enjoy them. Netflix, Hulu, Amazon and Apple now offer shows and movies in Dutch, some of which include English subtitles so you can check how much you understand. You can also watch your favorite movies with Dutch subtitles.

Don't have Netflix, Hulu, Amazon or Apple? Try watching on YouTube or downloading straight from the Net. You can also check out free Dutch lessons on YouTube in your spare time. This is a good way to judge the stage your Dutch learning has reached. If you are a beginner, look for lessons that teach you how to say the letters and sounds of the Dutch alphabet. It will help with your pronunciation. (See the chapter on best Dutch TV shows).

Get Dutch-language music for your daily commute

Why not practice Dutch during your commute? Singing along to songs will help your pronunciation and help you begin to think in Dutch (not a good idea if you use public transportation unless, of course, you have a superb singing voice). Try to learn the lyrics.

You can get music in any genre in Dutch on YouTube, just like in English. I suggest the following for language learners: Martin Garrix, Hardwell, Eva Simmons, Anouk, Jan Akkerm, André Rieu, Marco Borsato and André Hazes you can also hear most of these on the Spotify Channel.

Listen to podcasts in Dutch

While you're sitting at your desk, driving in your car on your way to work, or cooking dinner at home, put on a podcast in Dutch. It could be one aimed at teaching Dutch or a Dutch-language podcast on another topic.

For learning conversational Dutch, try Coffee Break Dutch, (https://radiolingua.com/2011/10/lesson-1-one-minute-dutch/), which focuses on conversations for traveling abroad, like how to order coffee! If you are a true beginner, DutchPod101 (https://www.dutchpod101.com/) is another great one. They have all levels of Dutch for any student!

Duolingo (https://www.duolingo.com/) has also just added a great new feature called "stories": fun, simple tales for learners with interactive translations and mini comprehension quizzes.

CHAPTER FOUR

A GUIDE FOR THE COMPLETE BEGINNER

If you are a complete beginner, you can consider using this book as a guide on *how* to learn and *what* to learn to enable you to speak Dutch as painlessly as possible. This guide will hand over the keys to learning Dutch for any and all potential learners, but in particular, it is for those who think they might face more trouble than most. It'll be more than enough to get you up and running.

These are the main subjects we will be covering as you begin to learn *how to learn* Dutch. You will probably notice that I repeat the idea of motivation throughout this book. That is because it is important. It is one of the main reasons people fail to achieve their goal of speaking Dutch and give up before they really get started:

- **Motivation:** Defining your overarching goal
- **Step by Step:** Setting achievable short-term goals

- **Getting There:** Efficient Dutch learning resources for beginners
- **Fun:** Having fun as you learn
- **Ongoing Motivation:** Staying motivated as you learn

We will go over each of these subjects in more detail later, but for now, below is a brief overview.

Definition of Motivation: a reason or reasons for acting or behaving in a particular way.
Motivation is critical for learning a language. Good, motivating reasons for learning Dutch include:

- "I want to understand people at Dutch events."
- "I want to flirt with that cute Dutch person at work."
- "I want to read Gerard Reve in the original."
- "I want to understand people at my local Dutch delicatessen."
- "I want to enjoy Dutch soap operas or TV series.."
- "I need Dutch for work so that I can communicate with clients."
- "I want to be able to make myself understood when I'm on holiday in a Dutch-speaking country."

These are all great reasons for learning Dutch because they include **personal, compelling motivations** that'll keep you coming back when the going gets rough.

They also guide you to **specific, achievable goals** for study (more on this later), like focusing on reading or on the vocabulary used in conversations on the dance floor.

Here are a few bad—but rather common—reasons for studying Dutch:

- "I want to tell people I speak Dutch."
- "I want to have Dutch on my CV."
- "I want to look smart."

Why are these bad?:

These are very likely not going to be truly motivating reasons when you can't seem to find time to open that workbook. They also don't give you any concrete desire to pay careful attention to, for example, a new tense that you've come across and how it might allow you to express yourself better.

If looking smart is your honest reason for wanting to learn a language, perhaps you could just lie and say you speak something like Quechua, which few people are going to be able to call you out on. (If you are interested, Quechua was the ancient language of the Incas and is still spoken in remote parts of South America).

Learning a language is a serious commitment

It is rarely possible to learn a language without a genuine motivation for some sort of authentic communication. That does not mean it should be painful or boring. Throughout this book, I will outline methods that make learning Dutch fun and interesting. When you are interested in something and having fun you do not have to consciously **TRY**, and strangely, this is when you perform at your best. You are in the *zone,* as they say.

Step by Step: Setting achievable, short-term goals.
As in life, once you are clear about your overall motivation(s), these should then be translated into achievable, short-term goals.

You're not going to immediately get every joke passed around the *drenkplaats* (pub/bar) and be able to respond in kind, but you should be able to more quickly arrive at goals like:

- "I'm going to place my favorite restaurant order in perfect Dutch." We go over this in the chapter entitled "Navigating the restaurant."
- "I'm going to memorize *and use* three words of Dutch slang." We go over this in the chapter entitled "Partying in Dutch-speaking countries."

I cannot stress enough the importance of correct pronunciation, as this will form the basis of your learning experience. There are a lot of free online pronunciation guides, make the most of them. It is also a good idea, if you have the equipment to record yourself and compare it to the native speaker.

If you want to take it a step further, there are some very good audio books in Dutch published by Languages Direct They have a whole load of audio books specifically designed to improve listening comprehension. The books are graded for difficulty so that you can assess your progress with each book.

Talk when you read or write in Dutch. *Writing* itself is an important part of language learning so read out loud (paying careful attention to pronunciation) and write in Dutch as much as you can. Just like when you took notes at school, writing serves to reinforce your learning.

- Watch movies with subtitles. Imitate some of the characters if you want.
- Listen to Dutch music, learn the lyrics of your favorite songs, and sing along with them.
- Join a local Dutch group. You'd be surprised how many there are and how helpful they can be for new language learners. This will give you a chance to practice your Dutch with a native speaker in a friendly and helpful environment.

CHAPTER FIVE

FLUENCY

What is fluency? Every person has a different answer to that question. The term is imprecise, and it means a little less every time someone writes another book, article, or spam email with a title like "U can B fluent in 7 days!"

A lot of people are under the impression that to be fluent in another language means to speak it as well as, or almost as well as, your native language. These people define fluency as knowing a language *perfectly*—lexically, grammatically and even phonetically. If that is the case, then I very much doubt that there are that many fluent English speakers out there. By that, I mean that they know every aspect of English grammar and know every word in the English language.

I prefer to define it as "being able to speak and write quickly or easily in a given language." It comes from the Latin word *fluentum,* meaning "to flow."

There is also a difference between translating and interpreting, though they are often confused. The easiest way to remember the difference is that translating deals with the written word while interpreting deals with the spoken word. I suppose, to be pedantic, one should be fluent in both forms, but for most people, when they think of fluency, they mean the spoken word. Nobody has ever asked me to write them something in Spanish, for instance, but I am quite often asked to say something in Spanish, as though this somehow proves my fluency—which is a bit weird when you think about it as it is only people who have no knowledge of Spanish whatsoever who ask me that and I could say any old nonsense and they would believe it was Spanish.

The next question most people ask is: how long does it take to be fluent? It is different for every person. But let's use an example to make a baseline calculation. To estimate the time you'll need, you need to consider your fluency goals, the language(s) you already know, the language you're learning, and your daily time constraints.

One language is not any more difficult to learn than another; it just depends on how difficult it is for *you* to learn. For example, Japanese may be difficult to learn for many English speakers for the same reason that English is difficult for many Japanese speakers; there are very few words and grammar concepts that overlap, plus an entirely different alphabet. In contrast, an English speaker learning French has much less work to do. English vocabulary is 28% French and 28% Latin, so as soon as an English speaker learns French pronunciation, they already know thousands of words. If you want to check the approximate difficulty of learning a new language for an English speaker, you can check with the US Foreign Service Institute, which grades them by "class hours needed to learn."

CHAPTER SIX

FORGETTING

We struggle to reach any degree of fluency because there is so much to remember. The rulebook of the language game is too long. We go to classes that discuss the rulebook, and we run drills about one rule or another, but we never get to play the game (actually put our new found language to use). On the off chance that we ever reach the end of a rulebook, we've forgotten most of the beginning already. Moreover, we've ignored the *other* book (the vocabulary book), which is full of thousands upon thousands of words that are just as hard to remember as the rules.

Forgetting is the greatest foe, so we need a plan to defeat it. What's the classic Dutch-language-learning success story? A guy moves to Holland, falls in love with a Dutch girl, and spends every waking hour practicing the language until he is fluent within the year. This is the immersion experience, and it defeats forgetting with brute force. In large part, the proud, Dutch-speaking hero is successful because he never had any time to forget. Every day, he swims in an ocean of Dutch; how could he forget what he has learned?

Immersion is a wonderful experience, but if you have steady work, a dog, a family, or a bank account in need of refilling, you can't readily drop everything and devote *that* much of your life to learning a language. We need a more practical way to get the right information into our heads and prevent it from leaking out of our ears.

I'm going to show you how to stop forgetting so you can get to the actual game. The important thing to know is what to remember so that once you start playing the game, you're good at it. Along the way, you will rewire your ears to hear new sounds and rewire your tongue to master a new accent. You will investigate the makeup of words, how grammar assembles those words into thoughts, and how to make those thoughts come out of your mouth without needing to waste time translating. You'll learn to make the most of your limited time, investigating which words to learn first, how to use mnemonics to memorize abstract concepts faster, and how to improve your reading, writing, listening, and speaking skills as quickly and effectively as possible.

It is just as important to understand how to use these tools as it is to understand *why* they work. Language learning is one of the most intensely personal journeys you can ever undertake. You are going into your own mind and altering the way you think.

- Make memories more memorable.
- Maximize laziness.
- Don't review. Recall.
- Rewrite the past.

How to remember a Dutch word forever

You can consider this part of the book to be a miniature mental time machine. It will take you back to the time when you learned as a child does.

Kids have amazing brains. They can pick up two languages in early childhood just as easily as they can learn one. Early childhood also seems to be the key period when musical training makes it much easier to acquire the skill known as perfect or absolute pitch. And that's not all: kids and teens can learn certain skills and abilities much more quickly than most adults. In a way, it makes sense that the young brain is so "plastic," or able to be molded. When we're young and learning how to navigate the world, we need to be able to acquire skills and knowledge fast.

As we age, we lose much of that plasticity. Our brains and personalities become more "set," and certain things are harder to learn or change.

As adults in the rapidly changing modern world, where the ability to learn a new skill is perhaps more essential than ever, it's easy to be jealous of how quickly kids can pick up on things.

How does one go from being a baby, whose linguistic skills end with smiling, burping, and biting, to being a fluent speaker whose English is marked by appropriate diction, golden grammar, and a killer accent?

Normal, everyday children do this in about 20 months.

This brings us back to the question: how do children learn a language? And what lessons can foreign-language learners get from these precious children?

So, we're going to trace a baby's journey from babbling newborn to kindergartner. Along the way, we'll note the milestones of language development

Pre-birth

We used to think that language learning began at the moment of birth. But scientists in Washington, Stockholm, and Helsinki discovered that fetuses are actually listening inside the womb.

They gave mothers a recording of made-up words to play during the final weeks of pregnancy. The babies heard the pseudo-words around 50—71 times while inside their mother's womb. After they were born, these babies were tested. By hooking them up to an EEG, scientists were able to see images of the babies' brains when the made-up words were played.

To their astonishment, the babies remembered and recognized the words that were presented when they were in the womb.

You know what this suggests, right?

It points to prenatal language learning.

It turns out, the first day of learning language isn't when one is born, but 30 weeks into the pregnancy when babies start to develop their hearing ability. So, be careful what you say around a pregnant woman, ok? Somebody's listening.

0—6 Months

Newborn babies are keen listeners in their environments. They particularly like to listen to the voice of their mother, and they quickly differentiate it from other voices. They also learn to recognize the sounds of her language from a foreign one.

Baby communication centers on expressing pain and pleasure. And if you listen very carefully, you'll notice that babies have different types of cries for different needs. A cry for milk is different from a cry for a new diaper—although a flustered first-time father might not hear any difference.

Around the fourth month, babies engage in "vocal play" and babble unintelligible sounds—including those that begin with the letters M, P, and B. (This is when mommy swears that she heard baby say, "Mama.")

6—12 Months.

This is the peek-a-boo stage.

Babies pay attention and smile when you call them by name.

They also start responding to "Hi!" and "Good morning."

At this stage, babies continue babbling and having fun with language. But this time, their unintelligible expressions have put on a certain kind of sophistication. They seem to be putting words together. You could've sworn she was telling you something.

It will actually be around this time when babies learn their first words ("no," "mama," "dada," and so on).

By the 12th month, you'll have that nagging feeling that she understands more than she lets on. And you will be right. Babies, although they can't speak much, recognize a lot. They begin to recognize keywords like "cup," "ball," "dog," and "car."

And on her first birthday, she'll definitely learn what the word "cake" means.

1—2 Years Old.

This is the "Where's-your-nose?" stage.

Babies learn to differentiate and point to the different parts of their bodies. They're also very receptive to queries like "Where's Daddy?" and requests like "Clap your hands" or "Give me the book."

As always, her comprehension goes ahead of her ability to speak. But in this stage, she'll be learning even more words. Her utterances will graduate into word pairs like "eat cake," "more play," and "no ball."

This is also the time when she loves hearing those sing-along songs and rhymes. And guess what? She'll never tire of these, so be prepared to listen to her favorite rhymes over and over and over again.

2—4 Years Old.

There will be a tremendous increase in learned words at this stage. She now seems to have a name for everything—from the cups she uses to her shoes and toys. She gains more nouns, verbs, and adjectives in her linguistic arsenal.

Her language structure becomes more and more complicated. Her sentences get longer, and her grammar mistakes get slowly weeded out. This time, she can express statements like "I'm hungry, Mommy" or "My friend gave me this."

She'll start to get really talkative and ask questions like, "Where are we going, Daddy?"

By this time, you'll begin to suspect that she's preparing to ask ever more difficult questions.

The child has learned the language and has become a native speaker.

So, what are the lessons we can take away from children as foreign-language learners?

We've just gone over how babies progress to acquire their first language.

Is there something in this process that adult language learners can emulate in their quest to learn foreign languages? Well, as it turns out, there is.

Understanding this early childhood learning process has major implications for adult language learners.

In this chapter, we're going to peek behind the curtain and look even deeper into how children learn languages to reap four vital lessons.

Each one of these lessons is an essential part of linguistic success.

1. The Centrality of Listening.

We learned in the previous section that listening comes very early in the language-acquisition process. Babies get a masterclass on the different tones, rhythms and sounds of a language even before they see the light of day.

Without listening, they'd have no building blocks from which to build their own repertoire of sounds.

Listening is so important for language acquisition that babies don't fully develop their language capabilities without the ability to hear. Thus, we have the deaf-mute pairing. How can one learn to speak when one can't even hear others or oneself doing it?

In addition, children who suffer hearing problems early in life experience delays in their expressive and receptive communication skills. Their vocabulary develops slower, and they often have difficulty understanding abstract words (e.g., extreme, eager, and pointless). Their sentences are also shorter and simpler.

In general, the greater the hearing loss, the poorer the children do in academic evaluations.

Listening is central to language.

It's the first language skill humans develop.

And yet, how many language programs pound on the issue of listening as a central skill, as opposed to grammar or vocabulary?

Listening is deceptive, isn't it? It seems like nothing's happening. It's too passive an activity, unlike speaking. When speaking, you actually hear what was learned. The benefits of listening are initially unheard (pun intended).

Contrary to common belief, listening can be an intensely active activity.

So, as a foreign-language learner, you need to devote time to actively listening to your target language. Don't just play those podcasts passively in the background. Actively engage in the material. If at all possible, don't multitask. Sit down and don't move—like a baby who hasn't learned how to walk.

Take every opportunity to listen to the language as spoken by native speakers. When you watch a movie or a language learning video, for example, don't just focus on the visual stimulation. Listen for the inflections, tones, and rhythms of words.

It may not look like much, but, yes, listening is that powerful.

2. The Primacy of Making Mistakes

Listening to a one-year-old talk is such a delight. They're so cute and innocent. Their initial statements betray a string of misappropriated vocabulary, fuzzy logic, and grammar violations.

When a 1-year-old points to a dog and says, "Meow," we find it so cute. When his older sister says, "I goed there today," we don't condemn the child. Instead, we correct her by gently saying, "No, Sally, not goed. Went!"

We aren't as kind to adults. We're even worse to ourselves.

Ever since we learned in school that making mistakes means lower test scores, we've dreaded making them. Mistakes? Bad. And we carry over this fear when we're learning a foreign language as adults.

That's why, unless we're 100% sure of its correctness, we don't want to blurt out a single sentence in our target language. First, we make sure that the words are in their proper order and that the verbs are in the proper tense and agree with the subject in number and gender.

Now, something tells me that a ten-month-old has no problems committing more mistakes in one sentence than she has words. In fact, she probably won't admit that there's something wrong—or ever know that something's wrong. She just goes on with her life and continues listening.

Why don't we follow this spirit of a child?

We already know that it works because the kid who once exclaimed, "My feets hurt," is now galloping towards a degree in sociology.

As a foreign-language learner, one of the things you need to make peace with is the fact that you're going to make mistakes. It comes with the territory, and you're going to have to accept that.

Make as many mistakes as you can. Make a fool out of yourself like a two-year-old and laugh along the way. Pay your dues. And if you're as diligent in correcting those mistakes as you are making them, soon enough you'll be on your way to fluency.

3. The Joy of Repetition

When your daughter is around 6-12 months old, playing peek-a-boo never gets old for her. She always registers genuine surprise every time you reveal yourself. And she'd laugh silly all day—all because of a very simple game.

And remember how, when your children were around one to two years old and they couldn't get enough of those sing-songy rhymes? They wanted you to keep pressing the "replay" button while watching their favorite cartoon musical on YouTube. You wondered when they would get sick of it.

But lo and behold, each time was like the first time. They weren't getting sick of it. In fact, it got more exciting for them.

Repetition. It's a vital element of learning. If there's one reason why babies learn so fast, it's because they learn stuff over and over—to the point of overlearning.

Adults never have the patience to overlearn a language lesson, to repeat the same lesson over and over without feeling bored to tears. Adults quickly interpret this as being "stuck". This lack of forward motion is promptly followed by the thought that time is being wasted. They think they should quickly press on to the next lesson—which they do, to the detriment of their learning.

We repeat a vocabulary word three times and expect it to stay with us for life—believing it will now be saved in our long-term memory. Quite unrealistic, isn't it?

In the prenatal experiment where made-up words were played to babies still in the womb, each word was heard by the baby at least 50 times. (Is it really a wonder, then, that the baby, when tested, recognized the words?)

Repetition is vital to learning. In fact, many apps take the concept further and introduce the idea of spaced repetition. SRS (spaced repetition software) can be an invaluable tool in your language learning toolkit. Try out Anki (https://apps.ankiweb.net/), FluentU (https://www.fluentu.com/), or SuperMemo (https://www.supermemo.com/en).

Unless you're a genius with an eidetic memory, repetition will be one of your most important allies in the quest for foreign-language mastery.

Repetition can take the form of replaying videos, rereading words, rewriting vocabulary, re-listening to podcasts, and redoing games and exercises.

Keep on repeating until it becomes a habit. Because that's what a language ultimately is.

4. The Importance of Immersion

Immersion can actually push your brain to process information in the same way native speakers do.

And is there anything more immersive than a baby being born and experiencing the world by observation?

Think about what the baby is experiencing. She's like an Englishman suddenly being dropped in the middle of China without access to the internet.

Everything is new.

So, you use your innate abilities to make generalizations, read context, listen to native speakers, and imitate how they speak.

Everything is on the line. You've got to learn how to communicate fast; otherwise, you won't get to eat—even when you're sitting at a Chinese restaurant. It's a totally immersive experience where you're not learning a language just for kicks or for your resume. You're doing it for your very survival. (That takes care of the "motivation" part of your learning.)

There's nothing fake about a child learning a language. It's a totally immersive and authentic experience—all their early language lessons are learned in a meaningful social context. I have yet to meet a baby who learned his first language by enrolling in a class.

For the adult language learner, immersion can be experienced remotely. One way of achieving immersion is by getting exposed to as many language-learning videos as possible.

Another way is something we touched on earlier: **spaced repetition**.

Remember that time you crammed information for an exam?

(Don't worry, we've all been there.)

You, like many others, may have spent an all-nighter memorizing every page of your notes and trying desperately to make up for countless days you decided to hold off on studying.

While you may have performed well on the exam, think about how much you recalled a few weeks after the test date.

How much of that information did you remember?

If you're like most humans, the answer is probably not very much.

Cramming does not work, especially when learning a new language.

You can try, but unfortunately, you won't get very far if you try to learn the Dutch subjunctive tense in one night. Now, you may wonder, "If I was able to recall information so well at the time of an exam, why has it dropped from my memory soon after?"

Well, there's science behind this! Research proves that cramming intense amounts of information into our brain in a short period is not an effective way for long-term learning.

British author H.E. Gorst mentioned in his book *The Course of Education* that cramming is what "produce[s] mediocrity". What he means is that cramming doesn't provide us with the ability to think critically and effectively apply our knowledge in creative ways.

Yet cramming is still becoming more and more popular among students of all ages.

If it's so ineffective, why do we cram?

Fingers point to improper time management as the number one cause. If we better prioritize our time, we can more efficiently learn new information. By cramming, we may absorb information that can be easily regurgitated the following day. But say goodbye to that information because it's going to disappear at an exponential rate as time goes on.

Cramming trades a strong memory now for a weak memory later. Unfortunately, we sometimes cling to short-term gratifications and fail to strive for long-term benefits. Before you banish all hope for your memory, there's an alternative method to learning that may give your brain the love it needs.

In psychology, there is a theory of memorization and learning called the "spacing effect". The spacing effect is the idea that we remember and learn items more effectively when they are studied a few times over a long span of time.

So, is frequent repetition the solution? Not quite.

Since cramming is out the window, you may think it's smarter to study material over and over again. It's crucial to note that while repetition is important, not all repetition is created equally. You'll want to space out the repetitions each time you study a set of information.

But determining how long to wait in between studying can also be a tricky matter. If you practice too soon, your brain will begin passively remembering information, which will not stick over time. If you practice too late, you will have forgotten the material and have to spend extra time relearning it. Add to this the complexity of individual learning and memorization patterns, and you have a recipe for guaranteed memory loss.

Thankfully, there is the aforementioned software available today to help us pinpoint the sweet spot of optimal learning. Just when our forgetfulness dips below a certain level, these programs jump in and keep our brains on track.

Spaced Repetition Software

Spaced repetition software (SRS) computer programs are modeled after a process similar to using flashcards. Users enter items to be memorized into the program, and they are then converted into electronic "decks" that appear on-screen in a one-by-one sequential pattern.

Usually, the user clicks one time to reveal the question or front of the generated card. A second click will reveal the answer or back of the flashcard. Upon seeing the answer, the user then indicates the difficulty of the card by telling the program how challenging it was.

Each following card's order of appearance is not random. In fact, SRS programs use algorithms to space out when each card will appear again on the screen. Cards given "easy" ratings will appear later than cards given "hard" ratings, thus allowing users to spend more time studying the cards that are more difficult. The tough ones will show up more often until they are mastered, giving you the chance to actively learn them more efficiently than with other learning styles.

Using Spaced Repetition for Language Learning

To put this into context, let's pretend you spend an evening studying a hundred Mandarin words you didn't know before. You continue studying until you've completely memorized the words. Let's say it takes you an hour to do this.

Immediately after reviewing these words, your memory of them will be quite high. However, over time, you will naturally begin forgetting the material you learned. And since it was your first time learning these words, your use-it-

or-lose-it brain is more likely to ditch this new material at a faster pace. The new knowledge isn't yet considered important enough to be etched into your brain cells.

However, the second time you study the same words, it will take you less time to master the set than it did the first time. Perhaps this time it only takes you 30 minutes to memorize the hundred words. Congratulations! You've completed your first spaced repetition.

So, does this mean you'll have to keep repeating the information you want to learn for the rest of your life? Not exactly. While it does require long-term review to keep information fresh on our minds, the time spent on review becomes shorter and less frequent over time.

With each successive review, it will take you less and less time to fully recall the information. As you begin mastering a set of words, you'll find yourself whizzing through each card. Eventually, information will become so memorable that you know it by heart. This is when you know you're ready to move onto a new, more challenging deck.

Self-discipline Ultimately Trumps All

Remember, while these programs may have wonderful language-learning techniques, they won't be effective unless you have the self-discipline to use them on an ongoing basis. If you're still at a loss for where to begin with organizing your own flashcards, check out Olly Richards's

"Make Words Stick", a guide for language learners just like you looking to get more out of their SRS.

Make it a habit to open up and use the software mentioned above. If you set aside some time every day to do your SRS studying, you'll see noticeable results sooner than you might imagine.

If, like me, you sometimes want to get away from the computer and get back to basics, you can make your own flashcards and use them manually. You can buy packets of blank cards at the post office or at any stationery suppliers. Write the English word on one side and the Dutch word on the reverse. You can choose your own words, but here are some to get you started. If you want to know how to pronounce them (this is absolutely essential unless you are already acquainted with Dutch pronunciation), head on over here: https://www.dutchpod101.com/dutch-word-lists

week (n) fem week	Er zitten zeven dagen in een week. There are seven days in a week.
jaar (n) neut year	een jaar one year
vandaag (adj) today	vandaag om kwart over zes (6:15) today at 6:15
morgen (n) masc tomorrow	morgen om tein over tien (10:10) tomorrow at 10:10
gisteren (adj) yesterday	Ik heb gister een virije dag genomen. I took a day off yesterday.

seconde (n) fem second	voor tien seconden for ten seconds
uur (n) neut hour	Ik slaap elke dag acht (8) uur. I sleep for 8 hours every day.
minuut (n) masc minuut. minute	Er zitten zestig seconden in een minuut. There are sixty seconds in a minute.
kunnen (v) can	Hij kan rijden maar niet zo goed. He can drive, but not very well.
gebruiken (v) computer. use	De programmeur gebruikt de The programmer uses the computer.
doen (v) het doen. do	De vrouw is huishoudelijk werk aan The woman is doing housework.
gaan (v) go	ga rechtdoor go straight ahead
komen (v) come camera.	Het meisje komt naar de camera. The girl is coming towards the video
zien (v) see	iets zien see something

goed (adj)　　　　Groentes zijn goed voor je.
good　　　　　　　Vegetables are good for you.

slecht (adj)　　　　De man is slecht.
bad　　　　　　　The man is bad.

Leuk je te ontmoeten.
Nice to meet you.

Hallo.
Hello.

Goedemorgen.
Good morning.

Goedemiddag.
Good afternoon.

Goedenavond.
Good evening.

Goedenacht.
Good night.

Tot ziens.
Goodbye.

Hoe gaat het?
How are you?

LEARN TO SPEAK DUTCH · 77

Ja.
Yes.
Nee (n) neut
No.

Ik ben... (naam).
I'm... (name).

Maandag
Monday

Dinstag
Tuesday

Woensdag
Wednesday

Donderdag
Thursday

Vrijdag
Friday

Zaterdag
Saturday

Zontag
Sunday

That should be enough to keep you going for a while.

We will be returning to childlike learning in Chapter Thirteen—"Learning Like a Child," as this lies at the heart of learning without mentally cramming.

Children are new to the learning process. They constantly see and experience things for the first time. They pause to listen to noises, try things over again until they master it, observe language until they can speak it, and ask if they don't know what something means. As we grow, we identify other ways to efficiently gather information. However, with this, we sometimes stop paying attention to the details in our everyday lives that can provide us with fresh insight and information. Consider these tips on how to rekindle this childlike process for obtaining knowledge.

Take Time to Observe
Start paying more attention to the things around you. Take time to appreciate the clouds in the sky. Pay attention to how your coworker's, partner's, child's day is going. Become aware of the people you are in line with at the checkout counter. Have a purpose in your observation, whether it's to better understand human nature, be more effective with your time, or gain an appreciation for others.

Go Exploring
Coming across things you have not seen or experienced before can help you appreciate things like a child would. Hike on a new trail, visit a place you've never been, or try a different route to work. Look at the things you see every

day with a new eye. Consider how you would perceive them if it was the first time you'd ever noticed them.

Learn from Everyday Moments

Pause to think about the things you do every day. This can be a good practice if you feel you don't have much opportunity to learn new things or if you feel you are not progressing in your education. Assess what you have learned during your day. For instance, did a conversation not go as well as you planned? Evaluate what went well and what could have been different. Consider how you can avoid a similar situation in the future. Write down the knowledge you have gained in a journal and review it occasionally. See where you have made improvements and how you have grown from these experiences. Note: This also helps with motivation.

Model Other People's Good Qualities

Start paying attention to the good qualities in others. Make a list of these traits and determine how you can emulate them. Work on the qualities one by one until you master them.

Take Time to Read

If you are busy, which most people are, look for ways you can incorporate reading into your schedule. Note: Unless you do not mind having to use a dictionary every minute, read dual-language Dutch books (the translation sits alongside the page you are reading). These are a brilliant learning tool and hugely enjoyable. You will extend your vocabulary marvelously without even noticing.

Listen to audio books in your car, read on the bus, take a couple minutes of your lunch break, or put a book next to your bed where you can read a couple pages before you go to sleep. Or, to start you off, here are some Dutch/English parallel texts you can try online for free:

https://www.lonweb.org/

Try different genres. Ask people what their favorite books are and read them—not only will you gain more knowledge from the books, but you will learn more about those around you by understanding the books they like. Study famous and influential people and events in history. Read both fiction and nonfiction. Do some research on the life of the author. Find out what world and local events were taking place at the time the book was written.

Talk to Others
Share with others the things you are discovering, whether it's something you read in the news or heard about in another conversation. By talking about what you are learning, you can better understand and retain the knowledge you gain. It can also help you discover fresh perspectives.

Be a Hands-on Person
Find a new creative outlet. Research how to prune rose bushes and practice on the ones in your yard. Follow instructions on how to cut tile and create a mosaic table. Take something apart to ascertain how it works. Enroll in a

continuing education course on NorthOrion, such as photography, ceramics, yoga, or bowling.

However you decide to do it, incorporate learning into your everyday routine. Select those methods that come naturally to you. Be willing to look at gaining knowledge as a child does, unembarrassed and optimistically. You may find that you can gain the same enthusiasm.

Please understand that when I say you should "learn like a child," I am not telling you to suddenly revert to wearing diapers and gurgling. I am talking about using some of the intuitive language learning processes that we use as children.

Adults have some advantages, which we will examine, and children have different ones. We can learn to use both precisely because we are adults.

One thing that is for sure: we don't have the same amount of time as children, so we need to optimize the time we do have to make time for language learning. But we can also utilize the time we spend doing mundane tasks to our advantage—listening to Dutch, for example.

The other thing you can't do is fully immerse yourself in the language (unless you are moving abroad, of course).

Your brain is nothing like a child's. The latter is a clean slate, and yours is like a graffiti-covered wall. So, when we want to learn a language, we have to clear our minds as much as possible. This is where mindfulness is so useful—more on that later.

Adults have a huge advantage insofar as first - and second - language acquisition are basically the same thing.

Adults are further advanced when it comes to cognitive development. What's more, they have already acquired their first language. It gives them the advantage of having pre-existing knowledge!

All these factors influence the cognitive structures in the brain and make the process of second-language acquisition fundamentally different from the ones occurring when you learn a mother tongue.

As an adult, you have the huge advantage over a child of being able to learn the most important grammar rules of a language when you want instead of having to acquire them slowly and through trial and error.

As I mentioned previously, adults have pre-existing language knowledge. Children have to learn the mechanics of their mother tongue, while, as adults, we have a more developed grasp of how language works. After all, almost all of us know what conjugations or adjectives are. What's more, adults are outstanding pattern-finding machines—it's much easier for us to deduce and apply language rules!

To sum up—as adults, we can learn really fast. But it all depends on how much we want to learn. **Motivation is key.**

Learning requires effort. We know that instinctively, and it sometimes seems that there is no way around it. The trick is to make that effort enjoyable; then it will no longer seem like an effort. It is just like someone who is happy with their job compared to someone who hates it. One will wake up in the morning looking forward to going to work, and the day will fly by; the other will dread getting up and drag themselves to work, and the day will also drag on interminably. Your language learning experience is up to you, and as an adult, you have the ability to make it as enjoyable and as challenging as you wish. It is a mindset. Once you learn to **see** your mindset, you can start to **choose** your mindset. As with everything—you will reap what you sow.

CHAPTER SEVEN

DUTCH GRAMMAR

Yes, I know, and I'm sorry, but you have to tackle it sometime if you want to master Dutch. Remember, if you are not interested in learning grammar (I can't blame you, although it makes things a lot easier in the long run), you can simply skip this chapter. If you prefer, skip it for now and come back to it later or learn it in bits—doable chunks. I actually recommend skipping backwards and forwards as you will find it easier the more you learn the spoken language.

If grammar really does get you down and you find it a hard slog, see the next chapter, which is on motivation.

Dutch grammar covers a lot of territory and I'm making a bit of an assumption that you're at least a bit familiar with English grammar because you're reading this in English. If it's your native language, you probably had some lessons about the difference between a noun and a pronoun even if it was years ago at school.

There is some good news though because many of Dutch grammar elements are similar to English ones.

Dutch grammar elements that are similar to English ones.

As is the case with many other languages, it's helpful to learn Dutch grammar by comparing it to English grammar. Like English, the Dutch language is based on subjects, verbs, and objects. That's one of the similarities, but it's really the differences that make learning a new language difficult. However, simple explanations can go a long way toward resolving that difficulty. For example, one of the differences between these two languages is that in Dutch, gender is assigned to all nouns. These genders are divided into male, female, and neuter. For example:

- Man (man), father (vader), and liar (leugenaaar) are all masculine.
- Woman (vrouw), mother (moeder), and knowledge (kennis) are all feminine.
- Forest (bos), girl (meisje), and Europe (europa) are all neuter.

That may seem a little confusing, especially when you notice that girl (meisje), of all words, is neuter! Fortunately, there are a few simple rules you can keep in mind to make life easier for you in this regard. For instance:

- If a word ends in –aar, -er, or –erd, then it's probably masculine.
- If it ends in –heid, -nis, or –schap, then it's probably feminine.

- If it ends in –the, then it's called a "diminutive," and it's neuter.

Articles are another area where Dutch grammar is similar to its English counterpart, in that there are three of them. Here again, however, there is also a difference. That is, the articles in the Dutch Language have multiple forms depending on the gender of their corresponding nouns. "De" and "Het" are both definite articles that mean "the." "De" is used with masculine and feminine nouns, and "Het" is used with neuter nouns. Here are three more examples to help you understand:

- de vader = the father
- de moeder = the mother
- het bos = the forest

Of course, just as there are definite articles, there are also indefinite articles. In English, these are "a" and "an." In Dutch, the indefinite article is "een," and it can be used with all nouns, regardless of gender.

Dutch grammar also has rules governing making words plural. Basically, you have to add "en" to the word. However, if the word has a long vowel sound, then you need to take out one of the vowels, and you need to double consonants that follow short vowel sounds. As with any other language, there are often exceptions to these general rules, but these observations will get you started. There are also rules about pronouns, adjectives, and conjugation in the Dutch language, and these are actually very similar to their corresponding rules in English.

Dutch Verbs

There is far more to learning the Dutch language than memorizing lists of vocabulary or developing your own accent so that you feel more comfortable communicating with native speakers. In order to be truly functional with the conversational elements of the language, as well as being able to read larger portions of text such as books or magazines, you will need to have a grasp of Dutch verbs.

Verbs are a critical element of language, and provide not just the action that moves a conversation or narrative moving forward but the context that allows a reader or listener to understand when and how that action is occurring in relation to the present moment. Being able to properly conjugate Dutch verbs will increase your ability to communicate effectively and naturally, and heighten your listening and reading comprehension skills.

The verbs of the Dutch language are not the simplest thing to learn. There are complex rules and conditions that regulate the usage of such verbs and because some of the forms do not translate into the English grammatical rules some people may find it difficult to understand them in the beginning. But, like learning your native language, consistent exposure and regular usage will help you to learn naturally.

Conjugation of Dutch verbs depends on, just as it does in English, the two grammatical numbers and three grammatical persons of the language. This means that there is a singular and a plural, and a first, second, and third person within the language. The grammatical persons are as follows, singular and then plural respectively:

First Person: ik, wij

Second Person: jij; gij; u, jullie; gij; u

Third Person: hij; zij; het, zij

Beyond the grammatical numbers and persons of the verbs in the Dutch language conjugation utilizes a variety of forms. The first to understand are the infinitives.

The present infinitive indicates that an action is being performed at that moment, and is formed by adding –en, -n, or –an to the root.

The future infinitive indicates that an action will be done at some point in the future, and is formed by placing "te zullen" in front of the present infinitive.

The present perfect infinitive indicates that a person is familiar with the action ("I have danced" as opposed to "I dance"), and is formed by putting "hebben" or "zijn" behind the present infinitive.

The future perfect infinitive indicates that a person while have become familiar with an action at some point in the future ("I am going to have danced"), and is formed by adding "te zullen hebben" or "te zullen zijn" after the present infinitive.

Gerunds

The verb form "gerund" refers to the situations in which the verb in used as a noun. In these situations the words are always singular and do not have a male or female inclination.

Participles

There are four participles as can be applied to Dutch verbs. These are:

The present participle

The future participle

The perfect participle

The perfect future participle

Indicative

In Dutch the indicative is the most commonly used verb form. This is the form that indicates the party that is performing the action. There are several such forms:

The simple present tense

The simple past tense

The simple future tense

The simple past future tense

The present perfect tense

The past perfect tense

The future perfect tense

The past future perfect tense

Neither the simple past future tense nor the past future perfect tense exists in the English language.

Other forms of verb conjugation are more complex and involve irregular forms and mixed verbs. Understanding these tenses will likely not occur until later in your language study.

Three Things to Keep Learning Dutch Grammar

1. Learn the gender of every new noun you learn

Much of the structure of Dutch grammar is based on whether a specific word is masculine, feminine or neutral. That fact affects adjectives, articles and your general sanity. So as you learn words, be sure to note the genders.

You can use different colors for different genders, you can put them in charts, you can invent mnemonic devices, or you can do whatever else works for you—just be sure to do it.

2. Learn the basic parts of speech

Strangely, learning Dutch grammar will also help you with English grammar.

You don't need to know everything, though. If you're unsure about the difference between a subordinating conjunction and a coordinating conjunction, you'll probably be OK unless you're a teacher or a grammar textbook author, in other words you are a normal human being.

But at a minimum, it's best to brush up on these ideas:

- noun
- pronoun
- adjective
- verb
- preposition
- participle
- definite and indefinite articles

You should also familiarize yourself with the idea of an **auxiliary verb**, **conjugation** and the concept of **tenses**.

3. Monitor your progress and be consistent

This actually applies to many aspects of language learning, but it can be especially important for learning the nuts and bolts of a language.

If you want to learn something new, you'll have to dedicate time to it. The more time, the better, and the more consistent you are with that time, the better. But if you can only do 20 minutes a day, four days a week, that's still probably more effective than 90 minutes in one breakneck Dutch-cramming session. Your brain needs time to absorb what you've learned.

One good resource for learning Dutch grammar at your own pace is: https://ielanguages.com/dutch.html. It gives you an overview of the Dutch language, including grammar, with sample sentences, images and native speaker audio to help you put the concepts you learn into context.

At the same time, record new vocabulary, new questions and new thoughts in some way. If you like to listen to music or watch classic movies, (go to FluentU where they have classic Dutch movies which are ideal for learning Dutch) you may still learn well, but most people find that by writing down new vocabulary words, for example, they retain a lot more of the new vocabulary that they've been learning. It also lets them monitor how far they've come and identify areas for future learning.

CHAPTER EIGHT

MOTIVATION *(yawn)*

I don't know about you, but I usually need some pretty strong motivation just to get out of bed in the morning. Maybe, its age... But I'm wandering off topic (onset of senility, no doubt). With me, it's usually the slow dawning of hunger and the yearning for caffeine, usually in tea form. If I can be bothered, I make it with (proper) loose tea in a teapot and pour it in to a bone china cup with a saucer. Why do I sometimes make it with a teabag in a mug and sometimes in a teapot and served in a china cup and saucer (a Royal Albert tea service if you must know). Well, for one thing, it tastes a lot better when I make it with "proper" brewed tea and serve it in chinaware, but that really isn't the answer, as just dropping a teabag in a mug still produces a good cup of tea and saves a hell of a lot of time and messing about. The answer is really that when I can be bothered to make *real* tea it is usually tied in with that thing called "motivation".

I do have specific reasons for choosing to make real tea most mornings, which I will not bore you with. Some are practical and others are sentimental. The mornings when I don't make real tea also have their own fewer specific reasons, usually involving lack of time, or simply that I can't be bothered.

Sit back for a moment with pen and paper and list the reasons you would like to be able to speak Dutch. Some reasons will spring readily to mind and will go at the top of your list, but others you might have to search a little deeper for and these are equally important. Have the list at hand, on a bedside table, perhaps, and give it a glance before going to sleep and upon awakening. The list may change after a while, but the reasons will be equally as important. They are your motivation, and you should reinforce them every day.

You don't have to use the same list all the time and writing it is just as important as reading it. Here is one that helps you to be positive about what you are doing. It is quite long as I have illustrated each point with an explanation, which you won't have to do as you will know what you mean. Feel free to take what you want from the list for your own use but don't forget to add your own. Only you know what really motivates you. I am indebted to Henrik Edberg from The Positivity Blog for the following list.

Get started and let the motivation catch up.
If you want to work in a consistent way every day, then sometimes you have to get going despite not feeling motivated. The funny thing I've discovered is that after I've worked for a while, things feel easier and easier, and the motivation catches up with me.

Start small if big leads to procrastination.

If a project or task feels too big and daunting, don't let that lead you into procrastination. Instead, break it down into small steps and then take just one of them to start moving forward.

Start tiny if a small step doesn't work.
If breaking it down and taking a small step still leads you to procrastinate, then go even smaller. Take just a tiny one-to-two minute step forward.

Reduce the daily distractions.
Shut the door to your office or where you are learning. Put your smart-phone on silent mode. If you are a serial web surfer use an extension for your browser like StayFocusd to keep yourself on track.

Get accountability from people in your life.
Tell your friends and family what you are doing. Ask one or more to regularly check up on you and your progress. By doing this, you'll be a lot less likely to weasel out of things or give up at the first obstacle.

Get motivation from people in your life.
Spend less time with negative people. Instead, spend more of the time you have now freed up with enthuasiastic or motivated people and let their energy flow over to you.

Get motivation from people you don't know.
Don't limit yourself to just motivation you can get from the people closest to you. There is a ton of motivating

books, podcasts, blogs, and success stories out there that you can tap into to up or renew your motivation.

Play music that gives you energy.

One of the simplest things to do when you are low in energy or motivation is to play music that is upbeat and/or inspires in some way. In the case of learning Dutch, play some Dutch music that have lyrics. There are also a lot of Dutch-speaking radio stations online. I will come to those later, but for the moment, you can just run a search on Google and choose one that suits your tastes.

Find the optimism.

A positive and constructive way of looking at things can energize and recharge your motivation. So, when you're in what looks like a negative situation, ask yourself questions like, "What's one thing that's good about this?" and, "What's one hidden opportunity here?"

Be kind to yourself when you stumble.

Don't fall into the trap of beating yourself when you stumble or fail. You'll just feel worse and less motivated. Instead, try this the next time: be kind to yourself, nudge yourself back on the path you were on, and take one small step forward.

Be constructive about the failures.

When you stumble ask yourself, "What's one thing I can learn from this setback?" Then keep that lesson in mind and take action on it to improve what you do.

Compare yourself to yourself.

See how far you've come instead of deflating yourself and your motivation by comparing yourself to others who are so far ahead of you.

Compete in a friendly way.

If you have a friend also learning Dutch make it a friendly competition to learn some task first. The element of competition tends to liven things up. You could also add a small prize for extra motivation and to spice things up.

Remind yourself why.

When you're feeling unmotivated it's easy to lose sight of why you're doing something, so take two minutes and write down your top three reasons for wanting to learn Dutch. Put that note where you'll see it every day.

Remember what you're moving away from.

Motivate yourself to get going by looking at the negative impact of not learning another language. Imagine where you will be in a year if you continue to learn. Imagine where you will be in five years if you continue to learn. Don't throw it away by giving up.

Be grateful for what you've got.

To put your focus on what you still have and who you are, ask yourself a question like, "What are three things I sometimes take for granted but can be grateful for in my life?" One possible answer could be: "I have a roof over my head, clean water to drink, and food to eat.

Mix things up.

A rut will kill motivation, so mix things up. Make a competition out of a task with yourself

Declutter your workspace.

Take a couple of minutes to clean your workspace up. I find that having an uncluttered and minimalistic workspace helps me to think more clearly, and I feel more focused and ready to tackle the next task.

Reduce your to-do list to just one item.

An over-stuffed to-do list can be a real motivation killer, so reduce it to the one that's most important to you right now (hopefully, learning Dutch), or the one you've been procrastinating doing. If you like, have another list with tasks to do later on and tuck it away somewhere where you can't see it.

Don't forget about the breaks.

If you are working from home try working for 45 minutes each hour and use the rest for a break where you eat a snack or get out for some fresh air. You'll get more done in a day and week and do work of higher quality because your energy, focus, and motivation will simply last longer.

Adjust your goal size.

If a big goal in your life feels overwhelming, set a smaller goal. And if a smaller goal doesn't seem inspiring, try to aim higher and make it a bigger goal and see how that affects your motivation.

Exercise.

Working out doesn't just affect your body. It releases inner tensions and stress and makes you more focused once again.

Take two minutes to look back at successes.

Close your eyes and let the memories of your biggest successes - no matter in what part of your life - wash over you. Let those most positive memories boost your motivation.

Celebrate successes (no matter the size).

If you're looking forward to a nice reward that you're giving yourself after you're done with a task, then your motivation tends to go up. So, dangle those carrots to keep your motivation up.

Do a bit of research before you get started.

Learning from people who have gone where you want to go and done what you want to do can help you to avoid pitfalls and give you a realistic time-table for success.

Take a two minute meditation break.

In the afternoons - or when needed - sit down with closed eyes and just focus 100% on your breathing for two minutes. This clears the mind and releases inner tensions.

Go out in nature.

Few things give as much energy and motivation to take on life as this does. Go out for a walk in the woods or by the sea. Just spend a moment with nature and, the fresh air and don't think about anything special.

What about learning a bit of Dutch while just laying on the sofa?

Coffee Break Dutch

This laid-back podcast does exactly what it says on the tin. The lively presenters give you ten-minute snippets designed to feel "like going for a coffee with your friend who happens to speak Dutch". The podcasts go through the basics at beginner level right through to advanced conversations and are perfect for listening to while snuggled up on the sofa with a cup of something delicious. The basic podcast version is free for all levels.

(https://radiolingua.com/2011/10/lesson-1-one-minute-dutch/)

CHAPTER NINE

BEST DUTCH TV SHOWS

Have you ever thought about learning Dutch by watching Dutch-speaking TV shows?

Instead of sitting in a classroom memorizing irregular verbs, you could be learning Dutch by sitting on the couch in your pajamas, munching popcorn.

But if it were really that easy, wouldn't everyone be speaking Dutch by now?

And come to think of it, wouldn't you have already done it?

Watching Dutch TV shows is a way of *adding* to your learning, but there are some pitfalls to watch out for. And you need strategies to make sure that you learn as much Dutch as possible while you watch.

In this chapter, we will look at the best Dutch TV shows on Netflix, Amazon Prime and Apple (if you do not have access to these platforms, you can use YouTube).

Learn how to make the most out of these Dutch TV shows. This includes:

- How to choose the right series so you'll get addicted to Dutch TV—and to learning Dutch!
- What to do when you don't understand (a common problem that's easy to solve when you know how).
- More than just chilling out: study activities to boost your learning with Dutch TV shows.

By watching Dutch TV shows, you'll constantly be improving your listening skills. And if you use the subtitles in Dutch, you'll also improve your reading and pick up vocabulary more easily. It'll even improve your speaking as you'll get used to hearing common phrases over and over, and they'll come to you more easily when you need them in conversation

Best of all, you'll be learning and enjoying yourself at the same time!

At this point, you might be thinking, "Sounds great, but I've already tried listening to Dutch TV shows, and I didn't understand anything."

And even if you do understand bits and pieces, watching TV in a foreign language can feel overwhelming. Where should you start? How do you know if you're learning?

By the end of this chapter, you'll have all the answers.

But first, let's look at the TV shows.

Beginners

Dutch TV show: *Buurman en Buurman*

("Neighbor and Neighbor") is a Czechoslovakian animated show about two clumsy but resourceful neighbors. In each episode, the neighbors do chores, but this often goes completely wrong in a humorous way. Because of the easy language and dry humor, it's fun for children and adults. The voices in this Dutch version are provided by Kees Prins and Siam van Leeuwen.

Note: This show is in Dutch, but the catchphrase "a je tol" is in Czech. It means "And that's it!" and the characters say this after their chores are "done." So don't confuse this phrase with Dutch.

Dutch TV show: *NOS Jeugdjournaal*

("NOS Youth Journal") is a Dutch television news program for children. It has a daily evening program, running every night for twenty minutes on NPO 3, as well as a short program in the morning during the week.

The *Jeugdjournaal* presents real news in language that young viewers can understand. Furthermore, the presenters and reporters speak very clearly. this makes it one of the best Dutch TV programs for beginners.

Dutch TV show: *Time to Dance*

Did you know that the Dutch have created some of the most famous talent shows worldwide? One of these great talents shows is *Time to Dance*. This talent show searches for the best dance talent in the Netherlands. Not much is said but a lot is felt, and watching this TV show is a great way to understand Dutch emotions.

The expert jury, which consists of Dan Karaty, Robin Martens, and Gianinni Semedo Modeira, judge individual dancers, duos, and groups, on their dance talent. The show has had one season on RTL.

Dutch soap opera: *Goede Tijde, Siechte Tijden*

("Good Times, Bad Times"), also called *GTST,* is the most famous Dutch soap opera. As it should be, this series is full of drama and therefore very addictive. It is one of the best TV shows for learning Dutch because you'll soon be hooked on the story, which revolves around family, friendship, love, and deceit.

The language is clear and the topics aren't that complicated, making it great for Dutch beginners.

Intermediate Learners

Dutch TV show: *Ik vertrek*

This television program follows Dutch families as they journey abroad. They move to another country where they, for example, start a hotel or restaurant. And as you can imagine, a move like this is not without struggles—but that's also what makes the program fun.

The participants may sometimes have quite a dialect, making their speech difficult to understand. however, once abroad, they'll also speak English, French, German, or whatever the language of their new country is. Who knows, you might even find an episode where a Dutch family is moving to your country.

Dutch TV show: *Toon*

This is one of the best funny Dutch TV shows of recent times.

Toon is about a hesitant composer of advertising jingles. The show begins with Toon (played by Joep Vermolen) coming home to find that his sister has organized a surprise party. Toon just wants a quiet evening, but people keep on asking him to play something on his guitar. Toon sings a song suggesting that his guests shouldn't stay too long at his party. The song is recorded with a cell phone and ends up on YouTube. The next day, the song has been watched by more than one million people and Toon is famous.

Toon is an easy and funny show that reflects Dutch humor. Therefore, it's a perfect way for the intermediate learner to get to know Dutch culture.

Dutch TV show: *Moordvrouw*

In the police show *Moordvrouw* (Literally "Murder Woman," but it refers to a woman who's really amazing or beautiful), a detective team in the province of Friesland solves murder cases.

The main character Fenna Kremer, played by famous actress Wendy van Dijk, is a scattered and impulsive inspector who tries to solve special cases with her colleagues. Other famous actors in the cast are Renée Soutendijk, Thijs Römer, and Porgy Franssen.

This is considered one of the best Dutch crime TV shows, sure to have you hooked. The clear language also makes it perfect for intermediate Dutch learners.

Dutch TV show: *Penoza*

The exciting drama series *Penoza* gives you insight into the Dutch organized crime scene.

Penoza tells the story of Carmen van Walraven (played by the great actress Monic Hendrickx), who finds out that her husband plays a very important role in the organized crime world. She forces him to stop; however, he is suddenly liquidated. Carmen then suffers from all kinds of threats, are which she chooses her one way out: she works towards the top of organized crime.

This TV show ran for several seasons on NPO3 and even has a movie. It's definitely the kind of show that will get you hooked, and you'll work hard to try and understand everything. Luckily, the language is clear and sometimes mixed with some English and Spanish.

Advanced Learners

These are the best shows TV shows to learn Dutch if you already have some knowledge and experience under your belt.

Dutch TV show: *Zondag met Lubach*

Zondag met Lubach ("Sunday with Lubach") is a late-night show with Arjen Lubach as the bold and thorough host. From behind his desk, Arjen reads the news from the past week in a satirical and playful way. He does this on the basis of excerpts from the media from the previous week.

Watch this show to learn more about the culture and dry humor of the Dutch. It may be a bit hard to understand sometimes, as it often refers to the Dutch culture and current affairs. But if you understand it as an advanced Dutch learner, you'll get to know the Netherlands better.

Dutch TV show: *De wereld draait door*

In *De wereld draait door* ("The World Goes On"), or *DWDD*, host Matthijs van Nieuwkerk has live converstations with well-known and less well-known guests in the fields of politics, science, sports, culture, and media. Talks can be about anything related to the news, information, or entertainment. Matthijs is always assisted by a famous co-host.

The program also devotes attention to music from the Netherlands and abroad. It's a great way to get to know the Dutch culture. However, be aware that they can speak very quickly (especially Matthijs) and there may be references to a lot of Dutch people you don't know.

Dutch TV show: *Undercover*

This Dutch-Belgium production, is all about Ferry Bouman (played by Frank Lammers,) one of the largest ectasy producers in the world.

Ferry lives a dream life in a country house on the border between the Netherlands and Belgium. But everything changes with the arrival of two undercover agents (played by Anna Drijver and Tom Waes) who try to disrupt Bouman's network.

This show is full of dialects, both Dutch and Belgium, so it may be a challenge to follow along. But the show is definitely worth it.

Dutch TV show: *De luizenmoeder*

De luizenmoeder ("The Lice Mother") is one of the best Dutch comedy TV shows, set at the primary school *De Klimop* ("The Ivy").

In the show, you follow the lives of the parents and teachers of this school. The director Anton (Diederik Ebbinge), the teachers, and the parents are all quite peculiar. This Dutch TV show is a great hit in the Netherlands because of its dry humor and bizarrity.

It may be difficult sometimes to understand its weird reference, but it will give you a (crazy and exaggerated) insight into how things (sometimes) work in the Netherlands.

For news on any new shows that are good for Dutch learners and language learners in general, go to my website: https://stephenhernandez.co.uk/ and sign-up for my monthly newsletter, or simply ask me through the Contact Form.

How to learn Dutch by watching TV shows

So now you've got some great Dutch TV shows to choose from. You can watch them as a beginner, but since they're aimed at native speakers, you'll probably enjoy them more if you're already at an intermediate level or above as you'll be able to understand more of what's being said and pick up new words without too much effort.

That said, it is possible to enjoy Dutch TV at lower levels, too; you just need a slightly different approach. In this section, you'll learn how to improve your Dutch by watching Dutch TV shows at any level.

You'll learn:

- How to choose the right series to get you hooked on Dutch TV shows (and, consequently, learn Dutch!)

- Study strategies to make sure you're learning lots of Dutch while you watch.

Which series should you choose?

The most important thing is to choose a show you really like. It's pointless choosing a drama/thriller like *Moordvrouw* if you don't like this genre. You'll get bored and drop it in no time.

Try to think about the kind of series you get hooked on in your native language and look for something similar.

How do you choose the right show for your level?

Some shows might not be the best option depending on your level. Let's take a popular show in English as an example: *Game of Thrones*. Being an epic story, it is a pretty complicated and demanding series, especially for beginners and "older" vocabulary is often used: words like "jester" and "mummer" which are practically useless at this stage. The fact that each episode lasts about an hour also makes it difficult to follow.

The best way to find out whether a Dutch TV show is suitable is by putting yourself to the test. Choose a show and play an episode with both the audio and Dutch subtitles on. Watch the episode for a few minutes.
If you can follow the Dutch TV show, great!

From now on, you will only watch this and other series with the Dutch subtitles on, listening and reading at the same time. This will help you memorize and see the usage of words you already know, and it will especially, help you understand what's being said by getting your ears used to these sounds while you read the words. If you find words or phrases you don't know, you can pause the episode and write them down or add them into a flashcard app like Anki (https://apps.ankiweb.net). Over time, this will become more and more natural, and when you feel comfortable enough, you may even abandon the Dutch subtitles.

If you found it was too hard to follow even with the subtitles on, don't worry; you still have some options.

You might struggle to keep up, either because

- There are too many words you don't know.
- They speak too fast.

If you are not already aware of it, there's an amazing Chrome extension that will help. It's called Language Learning with Netflix and has interactive subtitles that you can click on to get the definition in your native language. It also pauses automatically after every line to help you keep up. Give it a try—it could transform your Dutch!

Using a Dutch TV show as a study resource

If you find Dutch TV shows hard to follow even with the subtitles on, then start with a learner series.

One of the reasons Dutch TV series can be tricky to follow is that they're designed for native speakers—people who've spent their whole lives (at least 105,120 hours for an average 18-year-old) listening to Dutch. No wonder they're tricky for learners!

But thankfully, there are some series that are aimed specifically at learners.

Dutch Extra is a good place to start. You can find it on YouTube. Type in "Dutch Extra". Another option is to try using subtitles in your native language, just to get your ears more used to the new sounds.

One of the dangers with this technique is that you focus too much on reading the subtitles in your language and you don't benefit much from the Dutch audio.

One thing you can do to get around this is to pay as much attention to the audio as you can. You'll notice that many words and expressions are repeated quite often by the actors.

When this happens and you don't know them, write them down in your study notebook or add them into a flashcards app like Anki (https://apps.ankiweb.net/). If you can't identify the words by ear, write down what's written in the English subtitles and use a dictionary to translate it or just Google it. Alternatively, you can flip to the Dutch subtitles to see the expression written down.

In the meantime, keep studying Dutch and learning more vocabulary, and over time, you'll notice that you understand more of the sentences without even reading the subtitles anymore. At this point, take the test above again to check if you can move onto the Dutch subtitles phase.

Activities to boost your learning with Dutch TV shows

Sometimes, when you're watching Dutch TV shows, it feels magical. You're sitting there in your sweatpants, eating ice-cream and learning Dutch at the same time. It's a win-win scenario.

But then a niggling doubt creeps in... Is this enough? Shouldn't I be doing more to learn Dutch? While watching Dutch TV can do a lot for your listening and speaking, there are more focused activities you can do to accelerate your learning.

The best bit—they still involve watching some TV!

The reality is that TV and films help you speak naturally and understand more.

If you spend all of your time just learning the slow and stilted dialogues that you find in textbooks, you'll probably end up speaking in a slow and stilted way.

Alternatively, if you listen to lots of realistic conversations in TV series and films, over time, you'll start speaking in a more natural way.

The same goes for understanding: if you only listen to learner materials, you'll get used to hearing a version of the language that's been watered down for foreigners. You might get a shock when you hear people using it in real life!

On the flip side, if you get used to hearing realistic dialogues in TV series and films (even if it's tricky at first!), you'll be much better equipped to follow conversations in the real world.

I'm not suggesting you try to learn a language entirely by watching TV and films. Learner materials like textbooks and audio courses have their place in a language learner's toolkit. And as previously stated, speaking practice is essential to perfecting Dutch.

Foreign-language TV series and films are like handy supplements that can help you bridge the gap between learner materials and how people actually talk.

What if I don't understand anything?

When people think of learning a language by watching TV, they sometimes imagine learning through something akin to osmosis—the idea that if you listen to a stream of undecipherable syllables for long enough, it will eventually start to make some sort of sense.

But it doesn't work like that.

To learn, you first have to understand the language. Once you get to a high(ish) level where you can pick out a fair amount of what the characters are saying, you can learn a lot from just sitting back and listening.

What if you're not there yet?

Before that, if you want to learn a language by watching TV and films, it's important to do activities that'll help you understand the dialogues. The following activities will help you do just that.

How to learn a language by watching TV and films: what you'll need

First, you'll need a film, TV series, or YouTube video with two sets of subtitles: one in the language you're learning and one in your native language. This used to be tricky, but with YouTube, Netflix, Amazon and Apple it's getting easier and easier to find videos that are subtitled in multiple languages. Aim for videos where people speak in a modern and natural way (i.e., no period dramas).

One of the best of these is *Easy Languages* on YouTube. The presenters interview people on the street, so you get used to hearing natives speak in a natural and spontaneous way. What's more, the videos are subtitled both in the target language and in English.

Easy Dutch is particularly good as it has its own spin-off channel where they add fun and interesting videos a couple of times a week. If you're a beginner and you find these kinds of videos overwhelming (too many new words and grammar points), they also have a "super easy" series that you can use to get started.

Write what you hear

One super task to boost your listening skills is to use the videos as a dictation:

- Listen to very small pieces of the video (a few seconds each) and write down what you hear.
- Listen several times until you can't pick out any more.
- Compare what you wrote against the subtitles.
- Look up new words in a dictionary and write them down so you can review them later.

Often you'll see words and phrases that you understand on the page but couldn't pick out in the listening. You can now focus on the difference between how words are written and how people actually say them in real life.

This is your chance to become an expert at listening.

Make it your mission to become aware of these differences. Do speakers squash certain words together? Do they cut out some sounds or words completely? You may notice some things that native speakers have never realized about their own language and that teachers won't teach you.

Here is an example:
- In spoken English, "do you" often sounds like "dew," and want sounds like "one." So the phrase "do you want it" is pronounced like "dew one it."

No wonder listening is trickier than reading!

An awareness of these differences is your new secret weapon for understanding fast speech and developing a natural speaking style: the more you pay attention to these differences, the better you'll get at speaking and listening to the language as it's used in real life.

Translate it

Another invaluable task is to translate small passages into your native language and back into the language you're learning. After you've done this, you can check what you wrote in your target language against the original subtitles.

Ideally, you should translate the passage into your native language one day and back into your target language the day after so that you have to use your existing knowledge about grammar and vocabulary to recreate the dialogue (rather than just relying on memory).

This technique works because it gives you the chance to practice creating sentences in your target language and then compare them against the sentences of native speakers. In this way, you'll be able to see the gap between how you use the language and how the experts (the native speakers) do it. This will help you learn to express ideas and concepts like they do.

Comparing your performance to the experts' and taking steps to close the gap is a key element of deliberate practice, a powerful way to master new skills that is supported by decades of research.

Get into character.

One fun way to learn a language from TV and films is to learn a character's part from a short scene. Choose a character you like and pretend to be them. Learn their lines and mimic their pronunciation as closely as possible. You can even try to copy their body language. This is a great method for a couple of reasons:

- It's an entertaining way to memorize vocabulary and grammar structures.
- By pretending to be a native speaker, you start to feel like one – it's a fun way to immerse yourself in the culture.

If you are really up for it, record yourself and compare it to the original. Once you get over the cringe factor of seeing yourself on video or hearing your own voice, you'll be able to spot some differences between yourself and the original, which will give you valuable insight into the areas you need to improve. For example: does your "e" sound very different to theirs? Did you forget a word or grammar point?

Talk about it

A great way to improve your speaking skills is the key word method:
- As you watch a scene, write down key words or new vocabulary.
- Once you've finished watching, look at your list of words and use them as prompts to speak aloud for a few minutes about what you just saw.

As well as helping you practice your speaking skills, this method gives you the chance to use the new words you just learned, which will help you remember them more easily in the future.

Just relax and chill out

If you're feeling tired or overstretched and the previous four steps feel too much like hard work, you can use films and TV as a non-strenuous way to keep up your language learning routine. Get yourself a nice hot drink, make yourself comfortable on the sofa, put on a film or TV series and try to follow what's going on. Even if most of it washes over you, it's better than nothing.

While you obviously can't learn a language entirely by doing this, it's still handy because it helps you build the following four skills:
- Get used to trying to understand what's going on even if there's lots of ambiguity and you only understand the odd word (a useful skill to develop for real-life conversations!).

- Get your ears used to the intonation and sounds of the language.
- Become familiar with words and expressions that are repeated a lot.
- Stay in your language routine during times when you can't be bothered to study.

Don't underestimate the value of this last point: if you skip language learning completely during periods when you're tired or busy, you'll get out of the routine and probably end up feeling guilty. As time passes, it'll get harder and harder to get started again. But if you keep it up on those days, even by just watching a few minutes of something on the sofa, you'll stay in the routine and find it easy to put in more effort once you get your time and energy back.

CHAPTER TEN

NAVIGATING THE RESTAURANT

Who doesn't love to eat?

Explore delicious local foods while abroad—you won't be sorry! or if you are lucky, go to a Dutch restaurant in your home town.

Spending time at restaurants can really factor into your cultural immersion and Dutch language-learning experience.

Access to a fully equipped kitchen can be hard to come by while traveling, and you may well prefer to dedicate your time to seeing the sights rather than grocery shopping (though I'll be the first to tell you that exploring a local market can be extremely fun). Talk to locals, find out where the hot spots are, and ask about regional cuisine. People love to talk about food as much as they love to eat it!

No plans to travel? Join in on the fun by visiting a Dutch bar with Dutch-speaking staff.

You may be worried about your pronunciation, especially if you are not familiar with phonetic spelling. Don't worry; there are a ton of resources online that can help you hear and speak Dutch words. They are mentioned throughout the book and in the bibliography at the end. Use them and practice out loud as much as possible.

Alternatively, sign up for my monthly newsletter at my web site: https://stephenhernandez.co.uk/ for language-learning tips.

Some classic Dutch foods

Sure, you've heard of herrings, but probably the best herring dish in the world is: *Haring 'Hollandse Nieuwe'* (Dutch new herring).

Popular throughout the world, the '*stroopwafel*' is undoubtedly the most famous and popular pastry from the Netherlands. A '*stroopwafel*' is a unique kind of cookie. It is a waffle made from baked batter and sliced horizontally. The two thins layers of the waffle are filled with special sweet and sticky syrup (the '*stroop*') in between. The stiff batter for the waffles is made from butter, flour, yeast, milk, brown sugar and eggs.

A '*kroket*' is a deep fried roll with meat ragout inside, covered in breadcrumbs. The common English translation of '*kroket*' is croquette. The original Dutch '*kroket*' is made from beef or veal, but there are many different flavors like chicken satay, shrimps, goulash or even a vegetarian '*kroket*.' You can eat a '*kroket*' as a snack, but most of the time they are served on sliced white bread or hamburger buns with mustard on the side.

The Dutch version of French Fries has many different words: *'Friet'*, *'Frites'*, *'Patat'* or *'Vlaamse frieten'*. They are thicker than the normal French Fries and invented in the northern, part of Belgium. The Dutch really like them especially with a lot of toppings such as mayonnaise, tomato ketchup, curry or peanut sauce. A famous combination of toppings is mayonnaise, raw chopped onions and peanut sauce and is called a *'patatje oorlog'* ('fries at war'). It is tasty, but it does not look that way.

'Bitterballen' are the Dutch favorite snack and can be ordered in almost every café and bar, because of its real tasty combination with beer. These savory meat-based balls are deeply fried and traditionally served with mustard. The *'bitterbal'* has a crunchy breadcrumb coating with soft filling on the inside.

'Olliebollen' are traditional Dutch food. These treats are served at New Year's Eve and quite similar in taste to the donut. People make them at home during winter (holidays), but you can also buy them at the mobile stands on the streets in this season. *'Olliebollen'* are usually served with powdered sugar.

'Rookworst' is a Dutch smoked sausage. It is most often eaten with *'stamppot'* and mostly comes with *'erwtensoep'*. The taste is comparable to a hotdog, but *'rookworst'* is bigger and the

skin is crispier. '*Rookworst*' can be bought in every supermarket. Try one on a bun with a little bit of mustard.

'*Lekkerbekje / Kibbeling*'. This is the Dutch variety of fish and chips, but without the chips. '*Lekkerbekje and Kibbeling*' refer to battered and deep-fried white fish, commomly codfish or whiting from the North sea. The only difference between these two is that '*kibbeling*' 'is cut into chunks, while '*lekkerbekje*' is not.

'*Kibbeling*' is served with dipping sauces like a mayonnaise-based remoulade sauce (similar to tartar sauce) or garlic sauce. You can taste this delicious seafood at the same stands on the streets or market '*haring*' (herring) is sold.

'*Kaas.*' In this small sample of famous Dutch foods we have to mention cheese. The Dutch have been making cheese since 800 B.C. Furthermore the Netherlands is the largest cheese exporter in the world. With an average of 21 kilograms per year per person, we can say the Dutch love their own cheese. The Dutch eat cheese for breakfast, on sandwiches for lunch or as a snack (cut in cubes) served with mustard at the end of the day. It tastes great with a glass of wine or beer.

The majority of Dutch cheese are semi-hard or hard cheeses '*Gouda*' and '*Edam*' are the most popular cheeses from the Netherlands. But there are many other types of Dutch cheese.

I hope I've made your mouth water because the Netherlands is a smorgasbord of culinary delight (especially snacks). Each area of the country has dishes unique to that region, which can easily be found in local restaurants.

A note about tipping at restaurants in the Netherlands

In the Netherlands tipping is expected in restaurants for good or exceptional service, around 5-10% of the bill. if the service was average, you can round-up the bill or leave the change. Give your tip to the service person directly. You don't need to tip extra, but you can if the service was exceptional.

Before you arrive at your destination, equip yourself with the following words and phrases so you can order your meal like a native Dutch speaker!

- The meat is raw — *Het vlees is rauw*
- I like it medium — *Ik hou van half doorgebakken*
- I would like to try a regional dish — *Ik wil een gerecht uit de regio proberen*
- What ingredients does it have? — *Welke ingrediënten bevat het?*
- I like it rare — *Ik hou van kort gebakken*
- Well-done — *Goed doorgebakken*
- I have allergies to different foods — *Ik heb allergie voor verschillende soorten voedsel*
- What type of meat do you have — *Wat voor soort vlees heb jij?*
- This is dirty — *Dit is vuil*
- Can you give me some water — *Kunt u me nog wat water geven?*
- Is the fish fresh? — *Is de vis vers?*
- Sour — *Zuur*
- It is cold — *Het is koud*

- Can you bring me fruit Kun je me fruit brengen?
- That was delicious Dat was heerlijk
- Is it spicy? Ist het heet gekruid?
- Are they sweet? Zijn ze zoet?
- The food is cold Het eten is koud
- How is this prepared? Hoe is dit bereid?
- Grilled Gegrild
- Fried Getfrituurd
- Toasted Getoast
- Chopped Gehakt
- Breakfast Ontbijt
- Dinner Avondeten
- I am on a diet Ik ben op dieet
- I don't eat meat Ik eet geen vlees
- Baked Gebakken
- Roasted Geroosterd
- Sautéed Gemarineerd
- Steamed Gestoomd
- This is burned Het is verbrand
- Lunch Middageten
- Snack Snack
- I am a vegetarian Ik ben vegetariër
- I am allergic to nuts Ik ben allergisch voor noten
- Eat Eten
- Can I speak with the manger? Kan ik met de manager spreken?
- Tip Fooi
- How much do I owe you Hoeveel ben ik je schuldig?

- Do you have another credit card? *Heeft u een andere kredietkaart*
- Drink *Drinken*
- What is this? *Wat is dit?*
- Bill *Rekening*
- Can I pay with a credit card? *Kan ik met kredietkaart betalen?*
- The bill, please *De rekening alstublieft*
- I need a receipt *Ik heb een bon nodig*
- Where is the bathroom? *Waar is de W.C.?*
- Entrance *Ingang*
- Beef for the main course *Rundviees als hoofdgerecht*
- This beef is very delicious *Dit rundviees is erg lekker*
- Price of the order *Prijs van een bestelling*
- Select from the menu *Kies uit het menu*
- Non-smoking section *Niet-roken gedeelte*
- Smoking patio *Rook patio*
- Head chef *Chef-kok*
- Fast food meal *Fastfood maaltijd*
- Toetje *Dessert*
- Self-service restaurant *Zelf-service restaurant*
- Famous restaurant *Beroemd restaurant*
- Cellular phone bill *Mobiele telefoonrekening*

Dining out

When you're invited to a lunch or dinner, the Dutch will make it clear that you are their guest and that they intend to pay the bill, otherwise expect to "Go Dutch" and pay your fair share. No one will be embarrassed at splitting the bill. Dutch manners are frank—no-nonsense informality combined with strict adherence to basic etiquette.

A waiter or waitress is beckoned by raising a hand, making eye-contact and calling "Ober" ("Waiter") or "Mevrouw" ("Waitress"), but not too loudly. Another important point to make: snapping your fingers is considered very rude!

It is also considered rude to leave the table during dinner, even to go to the bathroom. During a long dinner, you may leave the table between courses to visit the bathroom. It is polite to ask if you may be excused. When you have finished eating, place your fork and knife at the 15:15 position on your plate.

As they say in the Netherlands, *Eet smakelijk!* (Enjoy your meal!)

Need help remembering these words? You can use an online resource like **FluentU** (https://www.fluentu.com/en/) to hear them given context and cement them in your memory.

FluentU offers a growing collection of authentic videos, including various clips, movies, music, and more. It's an entertaining way to immerse yourself in Dutch the way native speakers really use it while actively building your vocabulary.

CHAPTER ELEVEN

PARTYING

You're in the Netherlands, and you just got invited to a killer party.

Here are some words you should know before partying in the Netherlands.

Amsterdam is known worldwide for being a party hotspot. Many of Amsterdam's most popular clubs are located around the outskirts of the city, but nightlife in central Amsterdam is largely clustered in two major areas: the Rembrandtplein and Leidseplein both offer a variety of venues, including dance clubs, bars and casual clubs popular with local students.

Amsterdam has a thriving nightlife scene, with a "something for everybody" mentality. There are hundreds of bars and great nightclubs and music venues plus a long list of festivals in the summer. But if you're not careful, charges can add up quickly for everything from drink prices and cover charges to taxi fares back to your hotel. To keep your tab low, here are 5 pointers that will help save you wasting money when heading out for a night on the town for the first time.

If money is no object then (lucky you), feel free to ignore them.

Wine and beer have no fear

Much like the rest of Europe from Berlin to London, cocktail culture is a new phenomenon in Amsterdam and pricey at a typical cafe. Beer and wine are the usual orders and only cost a few euros.

If you are a beer person, stay away from pint orders. Bigger is not better in Amsterdam drinking, and the average Dutch pilsner will lose its freshness after any size above .33cl. If you're going for vino order the house wine, that's usually a nice French or Spanish pick that's smooth and easy to drink.

Trams before taxis

Trams and daytime buses stop running at around midnight—even on weekends. This makes taxis your only option when returning from a night out. Night buses are also available, but not very practical for visitors staying in the city center.

If you can brave bicycling back to your hotel or hostel, be careful and cautious. Otherwise know a walkable route before you let sobriety slip. In any case, getting a tram back means an early night out. Nightlife in Amsterdam can begin relatively early however, so calling it quits around midnight isn't the end of the world.

The clubs less traveled

Amsterdam's party hubs are Rembrandtplein, Leidseplein and the Red Light district. Here you will find many small clubs, most of them beckoning in the passersby with drink specials and a flashy storm of lights inside.

Here's a big tip for clubs in Amsterdam: you look for the club, the club doesn't look for you. The better clubs of Amsterdam, like Trouw, are on the outskirts of both the party squares and the city center. Be ready to drop about €25 for entrance, and once inside beer and wine are around €4 to €5, cocktails twice as much. And plan to cab it back home for another €25, as clubs in Amsterdam close around 5am on weekends.

Live music lovers should think small

Amsterdam has an amazing aura that draws national and international artists to the city on an nightly basis. If you're lucky, Paradiso or Melkweg will be hosting your favorite band at a smaller price and in a more intimate setting than back home.

Smaller venues like Winston Kingdom, Bitterzoet and Sugar Factory also carry impressive monthly programs at a lower cost, but of course the city has its fair share of free entertainment. Venues like Mulligan's Irish pub at Rembrandtplein, Jazz Cafe Alto at Leidseplein, and Cafe Skek near Central Station offer free music almost on a nightly basis.

Don't mix coffeeshops with cafes and clubs

Let's be honest, it's easy to go overboard with partying in Amsterdam. From the strong Belgian beers to the heavy marijuana joints and magic mushrooms, your vice(s) can run amok here. To keep a night out fun and safe, don't mix your party picks.

Know the basics. First, beers in Amsterdam start at 5 percent alcohol by volume and can easily hit 9 percent when dipping into Belgian ales. Be moderate with your partying, and you'll be able to enjoy Amsterdam pub culture more extensively (and vividly).

Second, smoking weed when you're intoxicated leads to black outs and vomiting for many many people. We all know that many dumb ideas sound great when you've been drinking, and that's one of them.

Third, consume cannabis with caution. Space cake potency is equivalent to four or five joints, and the highs can last for over 24 hours. Those wanting to purchase cannabis at a coffeeshop should inspect carefully what they buy. Many coffeeshops in Amsterdam have been caught lacing their products with chemicals and other substances to seem like a better deal.

Last, know that any hard drug that finds its way inside the clubs of The Netherlands are illegal, not regulated by the government, and the repercussions are serious. Have fun, but stay safe!

The Party Life in Amsterdam!

Ever heard of the phrase "Party Amsterdam"? Sure you have! If you are an unrepentant party lover, then the next stop for your 'partying cruise' should be the good old city of Amsterdam. The city is most commonly known as the party capital of the Netherlands for obvious reasons.

Amsterdam is a city with its preceding reputation virtually bigger than the city itself. The city is one that welcomes visitors with open arms, it even has pre-laid plans for visitors so they do not end up being bored during the course of their visiting period.

There are a large variety of activities to keep you occupied all through an ideal partying holiday in the city. The experience of these activities can be quite exhilarating. From having major fun in nightclubs down to experiences that are better experienced than said, the city is a field of enjoyable happenings eagerly waiting to be discovered.

Let us get on to the specifics of how to roll out the party life in Amsterdam!

Amsterdam's Nightclubs

The normal succeeding name that will follow the thought of having fun in the night irrespective is a Nightclub. Even beyond the city of Amsterdam, the nightclub is the most common way of having fun in the night, so why not also in our ever famous party city?

It is highly satisfying to know that there is a large number of a variety of nightclubs in the city. Standard nightclubs in the city are known to be open for business literally every day of the week. So if you are in the city on a quest to party away in Amsterdam, guess what? You are in for a fully satisfying period.

Each specific club in question have their own unique hours but it will definitely be between the hours of 10.00PM to 4.00AM. Information pertaining to each nightclub are best gotten from the club's personal site to avoid cases of misinformation.

As expected there are age limits for every club visitor. So if you are underage and on this quest of 'Party Amsterdam', you can as well remove nightclubs from your list. However, there is a little bit of good news on this topic. Different clubs in Amsterdam has a different age limit for access. Some clubs require that you are not any less than 21 years of age while some other clubs set their own age limit to people of 18 years of age and above, granting more access to people.

The dressing is another topic to be considered when planning on visiting night clubs in the city. As much as it is in the night and a club, it, however, does not allow the excuse for irresponsible dressing. All party lovers, specifically the night club lovers should ensure that they put in an effort to dress well at all time.

There are definitely entrance fees to be paid in order to be granted access into every nightclub in the city. These prices vary from club to club. However, for party lovers who want to enjoy the nightlife of the city but also do not want to break a bank in the process, there are the Amsterdam Nightlife Tickets to the rescue. This ticket helps you to enjoy admission to a number of Amsterdam popular Nightclubs and some special events for less money. With €10, you can gain access to the best nightclubs for 2 days in a row. A better option is to gain this unlimited access to the clubs for 7 whole days with a fee of just €20. With these extremely cheap rates, it is quite affordable to build life experiences.

The tickets even come with extra bonus plans such as a makeup touch for ladies at a specific studio before heading out for a night of fun. There are also bonuses of a certain rate deducted from your first Uber ride to cruise around the city. You can get free medium fries and drink that comes with the package of the Nightlife Tickets. There are a number of many other bonuses that come with this package.

Nightclubs to Party in Amsterdam

A lot of participating nightclubs for the Amsterdam Nightlife Ticket are located in the center of the city. The most popular party spots of the city can be said to include the Rembrandtplein and the Leidseplein. These spots are not really far from the city heart, so you can quickly head out there to catch the heap of fun activities going on there. A number of the city's best nightclubs are found in these locations and are also part of the participating clubs. There are about over 20 participating clubs, some of these clubs include:

The Club Escape Amsterdam

This is one of the happening clubs in Amsterdam. If you have been to Amsterdam and you have not yet been to the Club Escape, you should be questioned. Located in an easy to find place, the music from this club is one of very high quality and of all genres of music. If you came to the city of Amsterdam with just one intention, which is to party away every day, then you are in for a treat. There are even a number of weekly themed parties held during the weekdays so you don't have any excuse as to why you are not partying. When visiting the Club Escape, always remember to be dressed in your party best. Access into his club is from 21 years of age and above.

Supperclub Amsterdam

If you are a lover of R&B or the Hip-hop genre of music, then this is your best option! The Supperclub is one of the clubs included in the Amsterdam Nightlife Ticket but you still have not heard the best of it. The Supperclub has a number of other side attractions which would make you get even more of your money's worth.

A club combined with a gallery, this place is unlike any other clubs in the region. The gallery can be used to get into that same party Amsterdam mood without necessarily being physically involved. you can get to witness amazing hands down musical performances. The experience that can be gotten from this exciting stream of performance can only be imagined.

Another addition is the restaurant also located in this club. In this restaurant, you can get to experience a different kind of art in the form of food. You are introduced to a number of different striking culinary tastes which you cannot resist.

The Supperclub combines the restaurant, gallery and the nightclub to provide you with loads of experiences that you cannot afford to miss. You will get to satisfy your stomach cravings with food, satisfy your mind cravings with works of arts and most importantly satisfy your body needs by partying away the night in the club. In this club, you can choose to forget etiquettes, table manners and the likes. However, do not forget to ensure you are dressed right for the occasion so your partying vibes are not downed before they are even lighted.

The Netherlands is popularly known to be home to a number of big-time DJs whose names are known over the globe. DJs like the Afrojack and Martin Garrax are known to have their origin as the popular city of Amsterdam. Do you love the DJ kind of music supply? There is no better place to experience this other than the numerous clubs and partying spots in the city. Who knows you could get to meet another world-renowned DJ in your partying spree in clubs. Or you can even be luckier and actually get to meet these big guys in the industry.

The Melkweg Party Experience in Amsterdam

When visiting this famous country, ensure that you do not forget to visit the Melkweg. This spot was initially a sugar factory which was later switched to a milk factory and is currently used as a concert hall. This hall is located at Lijnbaansgracht and is one of the trendiest nightlife spots to include in your list.

The spot consists of a cinema, two music ballrooms and a café to grab a bite while waiting for your show. It has a predominant theme of pop culture which leads to having the same activities with regular night clubs. However, it also has unique events such as movie nights and exhibition among others.

Night lovers are always welcome to this spot and it is considered a favorite by many. At this spot, music lovers can choose to dance away to a variety of music all night long without the fear of being abruptly interrupted. Food lovers are also not disappointed as the restaurant located there is known to provide unique native food for its guests.

Amsterdam Dance Event

If you are planning your trip to the party city, why not give yourself a real party treat? Plan your holiday to fall around the period of the all-time favorite Amsterdam Dance Event and get to witness this mind-blowing exhilarating festival. If you think you are a fun lover, this is the perfect avenue to connect with other fun lovers like you and party away your holiday. The Amsterdam Dance Event (ADE) is known as the world's biggest club festival and also as Europe's leading electronic music conference.

Can you imagine having an unending diverse line-up of music playlist ranging from hip-hop to drum and bass to keep you moving? Yes, that's right! The ADE boasts of over 2500 artists from over 140 locations. There is a guarantee of 5 days non-stop partying for over 395,000 clubbers. This means that you get to also mingle while having your party fun.

The festival also has a number of side attractions, which includes the ADE playground which is a daytime program with a number of studio sessions, among many others. Ensure to plan your time well so you do not miss these five days of the festival.

However fun loving the city of Amsterdam is, it should be noted that there is a specific code of conduct to abide by when in the city. For instance, it is forbidden to drink alcohol in public places irrespective of your age. It is also not allowed to openly carry alcoholic drinks in some specific parts of the city. So a warning: breaking these specific codes can result in you being fined, and the Dutch are very organized and strict in that respect.

Here are some fun phrases and unusual names for things you can use when you go out in the Netherlands with their meanings:

To fall with the door into the house

Dutch : *Met de deur in huis vallen*

Meaning: To get straight to the point

As if an angel is peeing on your tongue
Dutch: *Alsof er een engeltje over je tong piest*

Meaning: Someone who is really enjoying their meal

Now the monkey comes out of the sleeve

Dutch: *Nu komt de aap uit de mouw*

Meaning: Similar to the English expression "to let the cat out of the bag"; the moment that a hidden motive or the truth behind something is revealed.

Origin: In the past, street artists would often perform tricks by hiding a monkey in their coats. At the end of the performance the monkey would "come out of the sleeve" and reveal the trick!

It's raining pipe-stems

Dutch: *Het regent pijpenstelen*

Meaning: Similar to the English expression "to rain cats and dogs"; to rain a lot. Since it rains a lot in the Netherlands, there are equally a lot of expressions about rain.

He who has butter on his head should stay out of the sun

Dutch: *Wie boter op zijn hoofd heeft, moet uit de zon blijven*

Meaning: Similar to the English expression "People in glass houses shouldn't throw stones". You should not criticise other unless yourself are without fault.

Origin: The phrase is said to have been around since the 17th century, as it was found in a text by the famous Dutch poet Jacob Cats (1577-1660). The reference is unknown, but it may refer to a time when people would carry their groceries in baskets on their heads.

To fall with your nose in butter

Dutch: *Met zijn neus in de boter vallen*

Meaning: To be at the right place at the right time

To buy a cat in a bag

Dutch: *Een kat in de zak kopen*

Meaning: To have been duped into buying something without inspecting it properly

Did you fall down the stairs?

Dutch: *Ben je van de trap gevallen?*

Meaning: A Dutch person might ask you this odd question if you have had a rather drastic haircut

Origin: The original version of the expression '*Hijs is van de trap gevallen en heeft zijn haar gebroken*' (He feel down the stairs and broke this hair) was already in use in the 18th century.

Hand shoes

Dutch: *Handschoenen*

Meaning: Gloves

Clean Mother

Dutch: *Schoonmoeder*

Meaning: Mother-in-law

Origin: The actual origin likely has little to do with the subject of cleanliness and more to do with the lesser know meaning of the word '*schoon*' meaning beautiful/fair. Similar to the French term belle-mere, *schoonmoeder* thus refers to your 'beloved' mother-in-law.

Toilet glasses

Dutch: *Toiletbril*

Meaning: Toilet seat

Origin: Some would say that the '*bril*' part comes from the shape of the toilet seat which resembles a spectacle of sorts hovering over the 'eye' of the toilet bowl. Another explanation could be it's referencing the 'shelf' inside Dutch toilets (instead of a water-filled bowl) which serves as a platter to display the contents of your bowels for closer examination. Yep, I'm grossed out too!

Peanut cheese

Dutch: *Pindakaas*

Origin: The oldest use of the Dutch word '*pindakaas*' dates from 1855. The word '*piendakass*' appeared in the Surinamese dictionary at this time and referred to a large block of crushed peanuts that locals slices in a similar way to that of a block of cheese and ate on bread. Peanut butter, as we know it, was introduced to the Dutch market by the brand Calvé in 1948. However, it was not possible to market it under the name of '*pindaboter*' due to the 'Butterlaw'. This 'Butterlaw' stipulated that only butter could call itself butter. Dutch peanut butter was thus marketed as '*pindakaas*'.

Nail pants

Dutch: *Spijkerbroek*

Meaning: Jeans

Origin: To understand the origins of this linguistic riddle we need to go back to the mid-1800 gold rush days when Bavarian immigrant Levi Strauss developed a pair of sturdy denim overalls for miners in San Francisco. Levi partnered with the tailor, Jacob David who suggested the final critical ingredient in making the pants even sturdier: nails! By bolting the material together at the seams with rivets the two entrepreneurs designed the perfect pants that we still wear today!

Butter ham

Dutch: *Boterham*

Meaning: Sandwich

Origin: While the origin of '*boterham*' is unclear, let me share this story with you. Once upon a time there was a man named John Montagu (1718-1792) who was a ferocious gambler. During marathon gambling sessions he was said to eat slices of cold meat between bread in order to avoid taking breaks to eat a proper meal. Mt Montagu happened to also be the Fourth Earl of Sandwich, thus the name of this odd snack took hold. As a footnote, I live a few miles away from Sandwich, a very beautiful and picturesque town and well worth a visit if you are in the UK, also, strangely, there is a little village called 'Ham' just down the road from Sandwich!

Donkey's bridge

Dutch: *Ezelsbruggetje*

Meaning: Mnemonic. A system of rhymes, rules, phrases, diagrams, acronyms and other devices which help you to learn and remember information. For example, most English-speakers know of the man named: Roy G Biv. The letters of his names spelling out the order of colors of the rainbow.

Origin: Donkeys are particularly fearful of water, so to get a donkey to cross the countryside it was often necessary to build temporary planks bridges over gaps and ditches, creating handy shortcuts. This is how *Ezelsbruggetje* came to mean memory tricks using shortcuts. Once a donkey finds his way over water the first time, it never forgets its route again.

Shield Toad

Dutch: *Schildpad*

Meaning: Turtle

Lazy Horse

Dutch: *Luipaard*

Meaning: Leopard

Sea Wolf

Dutch: *Zeewolf*

Meaning: Catfish

Belt animal

Dutch: *Gordelier*

Meaning: Armadillo

Garden snake

Dutch: *Tuinslang*

Meaning: Hose

Fire snake

Dutch: *Brandslang*

Meaning: Fire hose

Horse flower

Dutch: *Paardenbloem*

Meaning: Dandelion

To sit with your mouth full of teeth

Dutch: *Met de mond vol tanden staan*

Meaning: To be speechless

To walk on one's gums

Dutch: *Op zijn tandvlees lopen*

Meaning: To be exhausted

To sit like herrings in a barrel

Dutch: *Als haringen in een ton zitten*

Meaning: To be crowded

Origin: Fish are part of numerous Dutch idioms. For example, it is also not unusual to say someone is 'as healthy as a fish' (*zo gezond als een vis*). The herring, in particular is a traditional food and herring season is an annual event.

To have something under the knee

Dutch: *Iets onder de knie hebben*

Meaning: To possess in-depth knowledge of something, to master it.

Origin: The expression first suggested dominating an opponent in a fight and, over time, its meaning extended to things one can learn.

Cucumber time

Dutch: *Komkommertijd*

Meaning: This term refers to the quiet summer period when little happens.

Origin: Traditionally, farmers were busy during the summer months, but other businesses had nothing to do. More and more this term is used to refer to the lack of news or activity.

Talking about little cows and little calves

Dutch: *Praten over koetjes en kalfjes*

Meaning: Meaning that you are chatting about nothing of importance or nothing in particular.

I can't make any chocolate from that

Dutch: *Daar kan ik geen chocola van maken*

Meaning: Similar to the English expression 'It's all Greek to me'; indicating that you can't understand something.

What have I got hanging on my bike now?

Dutch: *Wat heb ik nou aan mijn fiets hangen?*

Meaning: This is a way of saying "What's going on now?" or "What do I have to deal with now?"

Origin: Cycling is the most common means of transportation in Holland. Many people go their entire life without owning a car.

We will certainly get that piglet washed

Dutch: *We zullen dat varkentje wel even wassen*

Meaning: That you will take care of something, fix something or get the job done.

Get a fresh nose

Dutch: *En frisse neus halen*

Meaning: To go outside and get some fresh air.

Now my wooden shoe is breaking!

Dutch: *Nu breekt mijn klomp!*

Meaning: To be totally amazed or not expect something

Kater

If you wake up with a "cat" the next morning, we're not talking about furry felines. *Kater* is the Dutch word for tomcat, but it also means "hangover." The origin of the word is twofold. While the chemical effects of alcohol can lead to feline-like moans, it may also stem from the Greek word for a cold, *katarrh*.

As with partying anywhere in the world it is best not to overdo it!

CHAPTER TWELVE

TRAVEL

You've bought your ticket, your bags are packed, and you can't wait to begin your journey to the Netherlands or many of the other Dutch-speaking countries spotted around the world. It should be remembered that outside the Low Countries, it is the native language of the majority of the population of Suriname where it also holds an official status, as it does in Aruba, Curaçao and Sint Maarten, which are constituent countries of the Kingdom of the Netherlands located in the Caribbean

Now, there is a simple thing you can do that can have a very big impact on your trip.

Learn some Dutch travel phrases!

Your trip will be so much more fun and meaningful if you can communicate with locals.

Below are the bare essentials, the most common survival Dutch travel phrases and words you will need on your trip.

Useful Dutch travel phrases every traveler should learn

Before you move beyond greetings, here is a tip for learning the words and phrases in this chapter: the best way to study them is to hear them in use.

Dutch greetings

Dutch-speaking countries are generally very polite, and you must always be courteous and say, "Hello" and "How are you?"

Do not worry about making mistakes; most people will try their utmost to understand you and to make sure you understand them. Just try your best, and they will be happy to reciprocate. Some of the phrases you will be already familiar with from earlier on in this book but there is no harm in revision (or to put it more plainly repetition)!

Essential short phrases

Good morning
Goedemorgen
khoo-duh-mawr-ghuh

Good day
Goedemiddag
khoo-duh-mih-dahkh

Good evening
Goedenavond
khoo-duh-nah-fohnt

Good night
Goedenacht
khoo-duh-nahkht

Hi / Bye
Hoi / Hallo / Daag / Doei
hoy / hah-loh / dahk / doo-ee

Goodbye
Tot ziens
toht zeens

See you later (in the same day)
Tot straks
toht straks

See you soon
Tot zo
toht zoh

Please
Alstublieft / Alsjeblieft
ahlst-ew-bleeft / ahl-shuh-bleeft

Thank you
Dank u wel / Dank je well
dahnk-ew-vehl / dahnk-yuh-vehl

Thank you very much
Hartelijk bedankt
hahr-tuh-lik buh-dahnkt

You're welcome (don't mention it)
Graag gedaan
khrahkh khuh-dahn

I'm sorry / Excuse me
Sorry
saw-ree

Pardon me (didn't understand)
Pardon, wat zei u?
pahr-dohn, vat zay ew

Yes / No
Ja / Nee
yah / nay

How are you? (formal)
Hoe gaat het met u?
hoo khaht ut meht ew

How are you? (informal)
Hoe gaat het?
hoo khaht ut

Fine / Very well
Goed / Heel goed
khoot / hayl khoot

So so / Bad
Het gaat / Slecht

uht khaht / slehkht
I'm tired / sick.
Ik ben moe / ziek
ik ben moo / zeek

I'm hungry / thirsty.
Ik heb honger / dorst
ik heb hohng-ur / dohrst

What's your name? (formal)
Hoe heet u?
hoo hayt ew

What's your name? (informal)
Hoe heet je?
hoo hayt yuh

My name is (I'm called)...
Ik heet...
ik hayt...

I am...
Ik ben...
ik ben

Nice to meet you.
Aangenaam (kennis te maken)
ahn-guh-nahm (ken-nis tuh mah-kuh)

Mister / Misses / Miss
meneer / mevrouw / mejuffrouw

muh-nayr / muh-frow / muh-yuh-frow
Where are you from? (formal)
Waar komt u vandaan?
vahr kawmt ew fun-dahn

Where are you from? (informal)
Waar kom je vandaan?
vahr kawn yuh fun-dahn

I am from the Netherlands.
Ik kom uit Nederland.
ik kawm owt nay-der-lant

Where do you live? (formal)
Waar woont u?
vahr vohnt ew

Where do you live? (informal)
Waar woon je?
vahr vohn yuh

I live in America.
Ik woon in Amerika.
ik vohn in ah-meh-ree-kah

How old are you? (formal)
Hoe oud bent u?
hoo owt bent ew

How old are you? (informal)
Hoe oud ben je?

hoo owt ben yuh

I am ____ years old.
Ik ben ... jaar (oud).
ik ben ... yahr owt

Do you speak Dutch? (formal)
Spreekt u Nederlands?
spraykt ew nay-der-lahnds

Do you speak English? (informal)
Spreek je Engels?
sprayk yuh ehng-uhls

I [don't] speak...
Ik spreek [geen]...
ik sprayk [khayn]

I don't speak ... very well.
Ik spreek niet zo goed...
ik sprayk neet zoh khood

I [don't] understand.
Ik begrijp het [niet.]
ik buh-khraip ut neet

I [don't] know.
Ik weet het [niet.]
ik vayt ut [neet]

How much is it?
Wat kost het?

vat kohst ut

I'd like...
Ik wil graag...
ik vil khrahk

Cheers!
Proost!
prohst

Have fun!
Veel plezier!
fayl pleh-zeer

Good luck!
Veel succes!
fayl suk-sehs

Be careful!
Wees voorzichtig!
vays fohr-zikh-tikh

That is great / terrible!
Dat is geweldig / vreselijk!
dat is khuh-vehl-duhkh / fray-zuh-likh

I love you. (informal)
Ik hou van je.
ik how fahn yuh

I love you (all).
Ik hou van jullie.

ik how fahn juh-lee
How funny / odd!
Wat vreemd!
vaht fraymt

What a pity!
Wat jammer!
vaht yah-mer

What is this / that?
Wat is dit / dat?
vut iss dit / dut

In pronunciation, kh denotes a uvular guttural sound. Meneer, mevrouw and mejuffrouw are all written with a small letter when they precede a name. When typing, de Heer is used instead of meneer and **Dhr.** is used on envelopes. Mevrouw and mejuffrouw are abbreviated as Mevr. and Mej. In addition, Mw. can be used as an equivalent of the English Ms.

Why you should learn Dutch travel phrases.

Even if you can't have a fluent conversation, native Dutch speakers always appreciate when foreigners put the effort into learning a bit of their language. It shows respect and demonstrates that you truly want to reach out and connect with people while abroad.

You won't be totally reliant on your Dutch phrasebook. Yes, your Lonely Planet Dutch phrasebook has glossy pages and you love getting the chance to use it—but you want to be able to respond quickly when people speak to you, at a moment's notice. After learning the Dutch travel phrases below, you'll only need your Dutch phrasebook in a real pinch.

If you can express yourself with some basic Dutch phrases, you are less likely to be taken advantage of by taxi drivers, souvenir shops and waiters!

The perception that all Dutch speakers speak English is simply not true. Even in the big Dutch cities you'll find loads of people that know very little English. You don't want to have to track down other English speakers every time you have a question or want to make a friend.

If you want to have an edge during your upcoming travels, take a moment to memorize the following Dutch travel phrases. You won't regret it!

Is there a bus from the airport to the city?
Gaat er een bus vanaf het vliegveld naar de stad?

Public transit is usually cheaper, if slower, than taking a taxi or rideshare. Use this phrase to see if you can get where you're going when you're strapped for cash, or just when you'd like to take the scenic route into town!

Is this the right bus for the airport?
Is dit de juiste bus naar de luchthaven?

Likewise, if you're the kind of person who can get themselves moving early (or maybe you just have a late flight), maybe you want to take the bus to the airport rather than taking a cab. If that's the case, you'll want to be sure you're actually heading the right way! You wouldn't want to end up at a lookout point half an hour away, watching your flight take off in the distance, would you?

Excuse me, what's the fare?
Pardon, hoeveel is de ritprijs?

If you are paying for a cab, you'll want to know how much. Most legal taxis will have meters, but when dealing with a currency you're not familiar with, it can be worth asking just to double check that you're paying the right amount – especially if the currency has cents.

I have a reservation.
Ik heb gereserveerd.

This one you can expect to use at least a few times throughout your trip, unless you're the kind of person who travels by the seat of their pants and just goes to whatever hotel, motel, or hostel has rooms available.

Do you have any vacancies tonight?
Heeft u voor vanavond nog iets vrij?

If that's the case, you'll definitely be using *this* phrase instead. Quite possibly a lot, depending on how lucky you are!

Where is the train station?
Waar is het treinstation?

If you're in a country with an expansive commuter rail system (or maybe just a fan of other types of locomotives), you may want to know where the closest station is. Just don't go looking for pennies on the rails!

I am allergic to peanuts.
Ik ben allergisch voor pinda's.

Replace "peanuts" with whatever the word for your allergen may be. If your allergy is serious, you probably already know the importance of stating this very clearly in Dutch.

If the condition is life-threatening, be sure to have a letter or prescription from a medical professional in Dutch on your person *at all times*. Consider getting a medical alert bracelet specially made in Dutch if your stay will be longer than a month or so.

Do you have any vegetarian dishes?
Heeft u ook vegetarische gerechten?

If you dislike eating certain things, or you have certain dietary restrictions, it would be best if you knew how to convey this clearly in Dutch.

Remember, though, that saying "I'm vegan" or "I'm diabetic" may not be enough to get you what you want. The rules for veganism and vegetarianism are not standard everywhere in the world. Also, your patron might not understand what "diabetic" means. If you have a medical condition, it would be best to research some in-depth vocabulary beforehand.

Could I get a map?
Kan ik een plattegrond krijgen?

Planning on exploring your destination? Hopelessly lost? Maybe just an amateur cartographer? No matter the reason, this phrase is sure to come in handy. That said, you're more likely to get use out of it at some sort of tourist or travel center than you are asking a random passerby on the street.

How much is this?
Hoeveel kost dit?

Even if you're not a big shopper, you're probably going to need this phrase at some point. Knowing how to count in Dutch will, of course, help a lot with purchases too.

Do you take credit card?
Accepteert u ook creditcards?

This is another travel phrase that will smooth your monetary transactions considerably.

Is the Wi-Fi free?
Is de Wi-Fi gratis?

If you're abroad, your normal cellular plans probably won't have any service, and you'll be totally reliant on publically available Wi-Fi while you're out and about. Just ask a server, clerk, or attendant, and they'll be happy to let you know. Just make sure you're paying attention when they tell you the password!

Could you take a picture of me please?
Morgen wij misschien de menukaart?

What would a trip be with no photos to commemorate the event? Just be sure to ask this of someone who actually looks like they'd be willing to, unless you're willing to risk being given the cold shoulder or worse. If you're at a tourist attraction, you'll find that most people are more than happy to take one for you, so long as you take one of them as well!

Do you have any recommendations?
Wat raadt u mij aan?

Eating alone in a restaurant? Or going out with new Dutch friends or business colleagues? Let them help you decide what to have.

I'd like to have a non-smoking seat, please.
Ik wil graag een rookvrije plaats hebben, alstublieft

Though smoking has gone out of fashion in some places, it's still popular in others. In the event you're at a restaurant where smoking is allowed on premises, you can always ask this question to the staff and be seated elsewhere.

Water, please
Water alstublieft

If you've emptied your glass, or are cutting yourself off after a few drinks, you can always ask for some water. It can be especially useful if the restaurant is busy to the point you need to call out to someone to get service.

Could I have the check?

Mag ik de rekening?

To finish off the restaurant related phrases, if you're eating with friends or really want to impress your colleagues, taking the bill can be a nice treat for them. Of course, this phrase could come in handy as well if you're eating alone and you're just impatient to leave.

What do you recommend for a sovenier

Wat raadt u voor een souvenir aan?

Now that your trip is over, what better way to cap it all off than a memento, or maybe a gift for friends and family at home? It'll be nicer to have something recommended by the locals than a cheap bauble from the airport store, so go ahead and ask someone you've met what they think.

When traveling, it's possible to keep communication smooth when you don't share a language.

Do so by keeping these five tips in mind. They are aimed to help you communicate with those who cannot speak English very well, and also to keep your traveling experience pleasant!

1. Keep your English simple and easy to understand.

If the person you are talking to speaks very little English, use basic verbs, adjectives, and nouns, and keep sentences short.

However, don't patronize them by talking in pidgin or like you would address a child. Keep your speech simple but natural, and use the correct grammar.

For instance, don't say: "You come when?". If you say: "When will you come?", you will very likely be understood, and may even help someone who wants to improve their English.

2. Ask someone to write information down.

Apply Rule 1 first at your hotel, where the staff is very likely to be able to speak some English. Get them to write down, in their native language, things like: "I would like to go to the airport, please," "Please take me to the beach," or "Where is the closest bathroom?"

These written questions are something you can then give to taxi drivers or any other people who are willing and able to help you. This simple step could make your life a lot easier when you travel to a foreign country!

3. Avoid asking leading questions!

If you want the correct information from a non-native English speaker, that is.

When you need directions, for instance, don't ask: "To get to the bus stop, do I need to turn left here?" If the person didn't really understand you, you will probably just get a smile and a "Yes," which could possibly make you miss your bus.

Rather, you should ask: "Where is the bus stop?" If they understand you, you will get the correct directions.

4. Pick the right person to ask for help.

Time to look at people and think a bit about their appearance! A younger person who looks like they might be a student is more likely to have English skills than the friendly but ancient lady smiling at you from a fruit stall.

If you don't see anyone like that, head into town to the nearest bank, hospital, pharmacy, or hotel. The staff at those places usually speak a bit of English.

5. Know when to quit.

If you stuck to the above rules, but the person you are talking to only stares at you blankly, say thank you and leave. Hanging around hoping someone will suddenly understand and respond is just wasting your time, and may irritate them as well. Go find someone else.

CHAPTER THIRTEEN

LEARNING LIKE A CHILD

As promised in Chapter Six, we are going to revisit what it means to *learn like a child* in greater depth.

Why is it that when we look back to our childhood, it seems that we effortlessly learned the things we truly wanted to?
There are a number of factors that we can look at individually.

- To start with, there seems to be a misinformed idea that as young adults, we have less on our minds and that this makes learning something like another language that much easier.

Mindfulness. Before you turn away in disgust and throw this book to the other side of the room shouting, "I knew it! He was a hippy all along. Now he is going to get me to cross my legs and hum OM," I am not going to ask you to do any of those things. If that is your thing, though, please feel free to do it, although I will remain dubious as to whether it will help you master another language.
I know mindfulness is a bit of a buzzword nowadays. A lot of people have heard about it but are confused about

what it really means. This is not a book about mindfulness, so I am just going to go over the basics. It means focusing your awareness on the present moment and noticing your physical and emotional sensations without judgment as you are doing whatever you happen to be doing.

The benefits of mindfulness are plentiful. It increases concentration, improves self-acceptance and self-esteem, strengthens resilience, and decreases stress. In a world where we are continually subject to stress mindfulness can provide an oasis of calm.

Mindfulness (being mindful of what you do), can also help you to learn a language much more easily because a part of mindfulness involves unconscious concentration. To achieve unconscious concentration as an adult we have to practice it, unfortunately, as it is a skill many of us have lost. It is not as difficult as it sounds, and in fact, it is quite fun. Just take time out, if you get a chance, and watch some young children at play.

Look at how hard children concentrate in whatever game they are playing. They aren't making a conscious effort to concentrate; they are concentrating naturally, thoroughly immersed in the game. This is mindfulness in its most natural form, and this is what thousands of people pay hundreds of bucks every year to achieve once again.

Now, see what happens if you get one of the poor kids to stop playing and ask them to do a mundane and pre-set task like taking out the trash. Watch the child's attitude change: she's now, not just annoyed and resentful that she has been taken away from her game, but the concentration that was there when she was playing has gone. You could say her mind's not on the job, and you would be quite right. The mindfulness has gone, but it will return almost instantaneously when she resumes playing and having fun.

Games, puzzles, and challenges are all fun to us when we are young and we devote all our mind's energy to them wholeheartedly, and that is what we will try to recapture as we learn Dutch.

When you are actively concentrating on learning Dutch, it is a good idea to turn off all distractions except the method you are using to learn. By this, I mean all the gadgets we are surrounded by, such as: the telephone, radio, Facebook, Twitter, Instagram—you get the picture.

Multitasking is one of those words that is bandied about a lot nowadays—the ability to perform lots of tasks at the same time. But in this particular case, multitasking is a bad thing, a very bad thing. It has been proven that it isn't actually healthy for us and we are more efficient when we focus on just one thing at a time.

Take some deep breaths and focus all your attention on your breath. You will find your mind wandering and thoughts will distract you, but don't try to think them through or control them. Bring your attention back to your breath. It takes practice, and like learning Dutch, if you do it every day, you will get better at it. Also, learning to breathe better will bring more oxygen to your brain.

Before you start any learning, take a few moments to breathe and relax. If you want, do some light stretching. This allows for better blood flow before studying. Better blood flow means more oxygen to the brain - need I say more?

When it comes to studying, do the same as you did with your thoughts: if you make a mistake, do not judge yourself Instead, acknowledge it and move on. Be kind to yourself at all times. You are doing an awesome thing - be proud of it. Remember that old saying: you learn through your mistakes. It is fine to make mistakes; just remember to learn from them and not get annoyed with yourself.

Just like with being mindful, be aware of the progress you are making with your language learning, but also be patient and do not judge yourself or compare yourself with others.

If you feel like it, smile a bit (I don't mean grin like a madman) as studies have shown that smiling brings authentic feelings of well-being and reduces stress levels.

You will find your mind wandering. Everybody's mind wanders. This is fine and completely normal. Just sit back and look at the thought. Follow it but do not take part. Be an observer, as it were. You can label it if that makes it easier to dismiss, for example, "worrying," "planning," "judging," etc. It is up to you to either act upon that and become distracted or let it go and focus on the task at hand - learning Dutch.

CHAPTER FOURTEEN

SPEAKING DUTCH

Learning Dutch vs. Speaking Dutch

Why do you want to learn Dutch?

This question was put to the students learning Spanish using an app called Verbalicity (https://verbalicity.com). This is what they said:

"My wife is from Mexico, and I want to talk to her parents who don't speak a word of English."

"I'm going to Guatemala next April, and I'd like to be able to have some basic conversations with the locals."

"We get a lot of Spanish-speaking patients at the clinic where I work, and I want to communicate with them better."

What did these people have in common? They all want to learn Spanish so they can use it in the real world. In other words, they wanted to **speak Spanish.**

Nobody ever wanted to learn Dutch so they can stay in their house and watch Dutch soap operas all day.

So, if the goal is to speak Dutch, then why do the majority of beginners start learning Dutch using methods that don't actually force them to speak?

This is the single biggest mistake that most people make when learning Spanish, Italian, French or Dutch or any other language.

Most learning methods only teach you the "stuff" of Dutch, like the grammar, vocabulary, listening, reading, etc. Very few of them actually teach you how to speak Dutch.

Let's compare methods.

Methods that only teach you the "stuff" of Dutch:

- Apps
- Audio courses
- Group classes
- Radio/podcasts
- Reading
- Software
- Textbooks
- TV/movies

Methods that teach you to speak Dutch:

- Practicing with people you know
- Meetups
- Language exchanges
- Lessons with a Dutch teacher online or in the real world

Many language experts, like Benny Lewis, have said that studying will never help you speak a language. The best way to learn Dutch or any language involves more than just studying.

Let's say you are learning to drive for the first time. Your parents drop you off at the driving school for your theory class.

You spend many hours learning about traffic lights, left turns, parallel parking, and the dreaded roundabout. Your brain is filled with everything you'll ever need to know about driving a car.

Does this mean you can drive now?

No!

There's a reason why they don't give you your license right after you pass the theory test. It's because studying theory doesn't actually teach you how to drive.

You need to be behind the wheel, you need to get a "feel" for it with all of your senses, and you need to get used to making snap decisions.

Languages work in the same way.

To learn a language properly, you have to speak it.

Speaking: The one thing that makes everything else easier

You might be asking, "How am I supposed to speak if I don't learn vocabulary and grammar first?"

While it's true that a small foundation of vocabulary and grammar is necessary, the problem is that most beginners greatly overestimate how much they really need.

People spend thousands of dollars on courses and many months of self-study and still don't feel like they're "ready" to speak Dutch. Speaking is something that they'll put off again and again.

Scientists from the NTL Institute discovered through their research that people remember:

90% of what they learn when they use it immediately.

50% of what they learn when engaged in a group discussion.

20% of what they learn from audio-visual sources.

10% of what they learn when they've learned from reading.

5% of what they learn from lectures.

This means that the best way to learn Dutch is to start speaking from the beginning and try to use every new word and grammar concept in real conversations.

Speaking is the one skill that connects all the different elements of language learning. When you are speaking, you are actually improving every other aspect of the language simultaneously.

Speaking improves:

- Pronunciation
- Reading
- Writing
- Vocabulary
- Grammar
- Listening

Here's a breakdown of how speaking can improve your other language skills:

Vocabulary

Have you ever studied a word in Dutch but then totally drawn a blank when you tried to use it in a conversation? Well, you will. Sorry.

This happens all the time because, although you can recognize the word when you see it or hear it, you can't naturally recall the word when you want to.

The only way for new words to truly become part of your vocabulary is to speak them repeatedly, putting them into real sentences that have real meaning. Eventually, the word will become a force of habit so that you can say it without even thinking.

Grammar

Let's say your friend asks you what you did yesterday, and you want to respond in Spanish:

>**What is "To walk" in Spanish?**
>"caminar"

>**Ok, time to use past tense, but should I use preterit or imperfect?**
>Preterit because you're talking about a single point in time.

>**What is the conjugation for "caminar" for the first person?**
>"caminé"

Your answer: "Ayer, caminé a la playa."

You may have studied all the grammar, but you would probably spend a good ten seconds thinking about this if you're not used to using grammar in conversations.

Speaking is the only thing that trains your brain and speeds up this thought process until you can respond in 1/10th of a second.

Listening

For many beginners, understanding native speakers is the number one challenge when learning Dutch or any other language.

When you are having a conversation with someone, you are speaking and training your ears at the same time. You are listening "actively," which means you are listening with the intent to respond. This forces you into a higher state of concentration, as opposed to "passively" listening to Dutch radio, for example, where you are simply taking in information.

Listening and speaking really go hand in hand.

Pronunciation

The first part of pronunciation is to understand how to correctly produce the sounds, which can be tricky, once you can do it right, the next part is about getting enough reps and saying the words out loud again and again.

Maybe at first, the words will make your tongue and lips feel strange, but over time, they will become part of your muscle memory until eventually it feels completely natural to say them.

Reading and writing

Dutch spelling is generally straightforward as most letters correspond to one sound, making it fairly phonetic to read. However, some people find the pronunciation difficult and think that Dutch sounds quite guttural. Dutch phonology is similar to that of other West Germanic languages, especially Afrikaans.

If you can say something in Dutch, then you'll have no problem reading and writing it as well.

However, the opposite isn't true. If you focus on reading and writing, it will not enable you to speak better.

Why?

Because, when you're speaking, everything happens in **seconds**, whereas reading and writing happen in **minutes**. Only speaking will train your brain to think fast enough to keep up with conversations.

80/20 your Dutch

Also called Pareto's principle, the 80/20 rule states that 80% of your results come from just 20% of your efforts.

This principle is absolutely huge when it comes to the best way to learn Dutch, and it has two major applications:

Vocabulary and grammar

Dutch vocabulary is predominantly Germanic in origin, with loanwords accounting for 20%. The main foreign influence on Dutch vocabulary since the 12th century and culminating in the French period has been French and (northern) languages, accounting for an estimated 6.8% of all words, or more than a third of all loanwords. Latin, which was spoken in the southern Low Countries for centuries, and subsequently played a major role as the language of science and religion, follows with 6.1%.

- The 300 most common words make up 65% of spoken dialogue
- The 1,000 most common words make up 88% of spoken dialogue

So, as you can see, you don't NEED to learn every single last word. Start by focusing on the most common words and the words that are personally going to be useful to you based on your interests and goals.

Just like vocabulary, you want to focus on the most common grammar rules and conjugations (ex. present, preterit, future, conditional, etc.). There are lots of advanced grammar rules that aren't used very often in everyday speech, so they are simply less of a priority.

Learning methods

It seems like there are a million ways to learn Dutch these days, from traditional methods, like textbooks, to endless online resources. This creates a big problem for language learners: a lack of focus. A lot of people try to dabble in as many as five or six different learning methods and end up spreading themselves too thin.

Instead, **choose the one or two methods that are most effective (giving you 80% of the results)** and ignore the rest. Let's start by outlining some of the methods you could choose for your Dutch learning.

Popular learning methods
Which methods work, and which ones should you not bother with? Here is a subjective low down.

The reasons why 99% of software and apps won't make you fluent

Take a second and think of all the people you know who learned Dutch or any second language.

Did any of them become fluent by learning from an app?

Packed with fancy features, there are hundreds of apps and software out there that claim to be the ultimate, game-changing solution to help you learn a language.

- "Advanced speech recognition system!"

- "Adaptive learning algorithm..."
- "Designed by German scientists."
- "Teaches you a language in just three weeks!"

But do they really work? Is an app really the best way to learn Dutch?

Or should you file this stuff under the same category as the "Lose 30 pounds in 30 days" diet?

The biggest software and app companies, like Rosetta Stone, Babbel, Busuu, and Duolingo, have all funded their own "independent" studies on the effectiveness of their software. In other words, they all paid the same researcher, who came to the conclusion that every single one of the apps was the best thing since sliced bread.

For example, the study for Babbel concluded:
"...Users need on average 21 hours of study in a two-month period to cover the requirements for one college semester of Dutch."

This is no surprise because the fill-in-the-blanks, multiple-choice, one-word-at-a-time approach of software is the same kind of stuff you would find on a Dutch midterm in college.

The problem is that just like software, college and high school Dutch courses are notorious for teaching students a few basics while leaving them completely unable to actually speak.

At the end of the day, software and apps, just like the traditional courses you take in school, are missing a key ingredient: speaking with real people.

The best and fastest way to learn Dutch is to spend as much time as possible having real conversations. It's the way that languages have been learned for thousands of years, and although technology can help make this more convenient, it cannot be replaced.

Software companies like Rosetta Stone have finally realized this, and in recent years, they've tried to incorporate some sort of speaking element into their product.

The verdict? Their top review on Amazon was one out of five stars.

Ouch! But if software and apps can't really teach you to speak a language, then why are they so popular?

Because they've turned language learning into a game. Every time you get an answer right, there's a little "beep" that tells you that you did a great job, and soon enough, you are showered with badges, achievements, and cute little cartoons that make it feel like you're really getting it. Of course, these things are also used to guilt you into continuing to use their app. If you stop using them, they start sending you pictures of sad cartoon characters telling you they will die because of your lack of commitment. Really? Do they think we've all turned into four-year-olds?

In the real world, playing this game shields you from the difficult parts of learning a language. You can hide in your room, stare at your phone, and avoid the nervousness that comes with speaking Dutch in front of a native speaker or the awkward moment when you forget what to say.

But the reality is, every beginner who wants to learn Dutch will have to face these challenges sooner or later.

The 1% of apps that are actually useful
Despite the drawbacks of software and apps, there is one type of app that can have a profound impact on your learning, and we have been here before:

Electronic flashcards (also known as SRS, or "spaced repetition systems").

I know I have already been over this, but they really do work. Ok, I know they don't sound very glamorous, and maybe the last time you saw a flashcard was in the hands of that nerdy kid in fifth grade that who nobody wanted to sit with at lunchtime.

But please, bear with me because this can totally change the way you learn Dutch. Here's how a flashcard system works on an app.

Each flashcard will show you an English word, and you have to try and recall the Dutch word. If you get it wrong, it will show you the card again in one minute, but if you get it right, it will be a longer interval, like 10 minutes or a few days.

A typical basic flashcard app is Anki. (https://apps.ankiweb.net).

Flashcard apps work by repeatedly forcing you to recall words that you struggle to remember, and as you get better, the word shows up less and less frequently. As soon as you feel like you're going to forget a new word, the flashcard will pop up and refresh it.

This system helps you form very strong memories and will allow you to manage a database of all the words you've learned, even those you picked up months or years ago.

You can also use flashcards for grammar concepts. For example, if you're having trouble remembering the conjugations for the irregular verb "hebben" (to have), just make each conjugation a separate flashcard, like this:

- Present simple > Ik heb
- Past simple > Ik had
- Present perfect > Ik heb gehad
- Pastperfect > ik had gehad

By putting all your conjugations in all the different tenses into flashcards, you now have a way to repeatedly drill them into your memory.

The major advantage of flashcards is that all you really need is 10-20 minutes a day: Every single day, we spend a lot of time waiting around, whether it's for public transportation, in line at the supermarket, or for a doctor's appointment. This is all wasted time that you can use to improve your vocabulary. It only takes a few seconds to turn on the flashcard app and review a few words.

If you want to try this out, these are probably the two best apps out there:

Anki (https://apps.ankiweb.net)
The original, "pure" flashcard app.

Pros:
- Reviewing cards is extremely simple and straightforward.
- Very easy to write your own cards; it can be done on the fly.
- Plenty of customization options and user-written decks to download (although not as many as Memrise).

Cons:
- It can be a bit confusing to set up; you need to be tech-savvy.
- It doesn't provide reminders/motivation to practice daily.

Cost:
- Free for Android, computer.
- US$24.99 for iOS.

Memrise (https://www.memrise.com)

Flashcard-based app with modern features.

Pros:

- More variety for reviewing cards (fill-in-the-blanks, audio recordings, etc.).
- Offers a little bit of gamification (rewards, reminders) to keep you motivated.
- It has a big library of card decks written by other people and a large community of users.

Cons:

- Writing your own cards (called "Create a Course") is not as easy as Anki and can't be done on mobile.
- The review system works differently from traditional cards.

Cost:

- Free for all platforms (iOS, Android, computer).

Both apps come with standard Dutch vocabulary decks as well as those written by other users. However, the real beauty of flashcards is being able to write the decks yourself. There is a big advantage to doing this, which you can see from the following steps:

When using pre-written flashcards

- You see a new word for the first time in your app and then review the word until you remember it.

When making flashcards yourself

- You get exposed to a new world through conversation, your teacher, or something you've seen or heard. You associate the word with a real-life situation.
- You write it into a flashcard, and by doing this, you're already strengthening your memory of that word.
- You review the word until you remember it.

As you can see, while making the cards yourself takes a bit of extra work, you get to control the words you learn and can focus on the ones that are more meaningful to you. Plus, the process of writing the word down acts as an extra round of review.

While it is true that flashcard apps have a bit of a learning curve, they are very easy once you get the hang of them, and you'll notice a huge difference in memorizing vocabulary and grammar.

Can you learn Dutch by just watching TV and listening to the radio?

Countless beginners have tried and failed to learn Dutch by what is known as "passive listening." Examples of passive listening include:

- Audio courses
- Radio and podcasts
- Movies and TV shows

The idea of passive listening sounds good on paper. You can learn Dutch by listening to an audio course in your car on the way to work. Put on some Dutch radio while you're making dinner and then sit down for an episode of *Hollands Hoop* while you fold your laundry.

Except this doesn't work. Why?

Because learning a language is an ACTIVE process. You can't spend hundreds of hours listening to stuff in the background and expect your brain to figure it all out.

Now, many people will have a couple of objections to this:

I thought passive listening is how babies learn languages?

Let's assume out of simplicity that a baby is awake for an average of eight hours a day for the first year of its life. Through all the feedings and diaper changes, it is constantly being exposed to language because its parents are talking to it (and each other). So, by the time a baby says their first words at around the one-year mark, it has already had about three thousand hours of passive-listening exposure (8 hours x 365 days).

Now, how do you compete with that as a busy adult? Even if you squeeze in an hour a day of Dutch radio into your daily life, it would still take you eight years to get the equivalent amount of language exposure. Who has the patience to spend eight years learning Dutch?

Don't sell yourself short. With the right method and motivation, you can learn the Dutch you need in months, not years.

If you incorporate a bit of Dutch into every aspect of your life, then that's immersion, right? Isn't immersion the best way to learn Dutch?

There are many expats who have lived in Spain or Latin America for 5-10 years, and guess what? They STILL can't speak a word of Spanish let alone form a sentence.

These people have the perfect environment to learn, they can hear Spanish everywhere when walking down the street, and every friend or acquaintance is someone they can practice with. But somehow, none of this seems to help.

Why?
Because they don't make an effort to speak.

Immersion is extremely effective, but only if you take advantage of the environment you're in and speak Dutch every chance you get. Simply being there and listening is not enough.

As an adult, we have to learn languages actively. Most of us want to go from beginner to fluent in as short a time as possible, and passive listening is simply too slow.

If you're already listening to a lot of Dutch, it doesn't mean you should stop. Try to do it actively, which means giving it

100% of your attention rather than having it in the background as you're doing something else.

Listening to radio, TV, and movies can be useful at a later stage. Increasing the amount of Dutch you hear will speed up your progress when you are already at a conversational level.

But when it comes to learning Dutch as a complete beginner, there are far more efficient methods.

How to practice Dutch

We've already established that the best way to learn Dutch for beginners involves speaking as much as possible. Let's go over the four main ways that you practice speaking Dutch:

Speak with people you know

Maybe you have friends who are native Dutch speakers, or maybe you are dating or married to one! If that person is the reason you wanted to learn Dutch in the first place, it may seem like a good idea to practice with them from the beginning.

Pros:

- It's free.
- Practicing with people you know can be less intimidating than with a stranger, and as a result, you might be more willing to open up and speak (although, for some people, it has the opposite effect).

- They know you, and they like you, so they will probably be very supportive and patient with you.

Cons:
- You may not know anyone in your immediate circle of friends and family who speak Dutch.
- When you make a mistake, they probably won't be able to explain what you did wrong. Most native speakers don't know the rules of their own language. Things "just sound right" to them.
- People have deeply ingrained habits. Once a relationship is established, it is really hard to change the language of communication. You can try to practice Dutch with your wife, who is a native speaker, but more often than not, you'll find yourselves defaulting back to English because "it's just easier."
- Trying to practice Dutch with friends and family can be frustrating. You're going to stutter, you won't be able to express yourself the way you usually do, and your wonderful sense of humor will suddenly become nonexistent. You'll feel guilty that you're being an inconvenience to them (although most of the time it's a bigger deal for you than it is for them).

Go to Meetups

Dutch learners often get together a few times a week at a public place (usually a café) and practice speaking for an hour or two. A good place to find them is Meetup.com (https://www.meetup.com). Just do a search for "Dutch + *the city you live in*."

Pros:

- It's free.
- You get to meet new people in your area who are learning Dutch just like you. Since you're all in the same boat, you can encourage each other and help each other stay accountable.
- You can share learning tips with each other, like what's working and what's not.
- If you need an explanation for a grammar concept, chances are someone in the group knows and can explain it to you.

Cons:

- You'll only be able to find meetups in big cities. If you live in a smaller city or town, then you're out of luck.
- It's not great for shy people. Speaking in a group of 10-15 people can be pretty intimidating.
- What often happens at meetups is that you all sit around a table and two or three people will end up doing most of the talking (remember the 80/20 rule?) while the rest just sit there and listen.
- Everyone is at different levels of fluency, so you could find yourself talking to someone who is way more advanced than you are, and you may end up boring them. Unfortunately, some groups don't let complete beginners join for this very reason.
- If you are just starting out and don't feel confident in speaking, you might end up doing a whole lot

listening and not much talking. You get much better value out of meetups if you are already somewhat conversational.

Language exchanges

The basic idea is to find a native Dutch speaker who is trying to learn English. You meet in person or have a Skype call (or something similar) where you split your time practicing both Dutch and English. The easiest way to find a partner is through online exchanges like My Language Exchange (https://www.mylanguageexchange.com) and Conversation Exchange (https://www.conversationexchange.com).

Pros:

- It's free.
- You can get exposure to a lot of different people who come from different Dutch-speaking countries and with different backgrounds.

Cons:

- It can be very time consuming to find the right language partner. It can take a lot of trial and error.
- You only get to spend 50% of your time speaking in Dutch.
- Your partner won't be able to speak English well, so it can be tough to communicate if both of you are beginners.
- Your partner probably won't be able to explain Dutch grammar to you, and you won't be able to explain

English very well, either. For example, can you explain when you should use "which" vs. "that"? Or how about "who" vs. "whom"?
- Partners can be flaky since there is no paid commitment, and some people simply don't show up at the agreed time (happens more often in online exchanges).

Professional Dutch teachers

These days it is far more convenient to find a Dutch teacher online, and believe it or not, this can be even more interactive than being face-to-face. You participate in your lessons via Skype from the comfort of home and on your own schedule. This is how many people prefer to learn Dutch.

Pros:

- A good teacher is like having your own coach or personal trainer. They want you to succeed, and they are there to support you and offer motivation and advice. It is much easier to learn Dutch when someone is there to hold you accountable.
- A teacher is a trained professional. They have comprehensive knowledge of both Dutch and English grammar, so they can explain to you the difference between the two, and provide a lot of useful examples to help you understand difficult concepts.
- Teachers know how to correct you when you make a mistake, but not so often as to interrupt the flow of conversation. Talking to a teacher just feels natural.

- Even if you're the shyest person in the world, a good teacher knows how to coax you into speaking and how to build your confidence. You don't have to worry about making mistakes, you'll no longer feel embarrassed, and ultimately, you'll have fun.
- A teacher can quickly figure out your strengths and weaknesses and come up with a learning plan to address them.
- They will design a customized curriculum for you based on your learning goals and interests. This ensures that whatever they teach will be very meaningful to you.
- A good Dutch teacher should provide you with all the materials that you'll need, so you won't have to buy a textbook or spend time looking for grammar exercises.
- While a good chunk of your time is spent having conversations, your teacher will introduce exercises that cover all language skills, including pronunciation, reading, writing, and listening.

Cons:

- Just like language exchange partners, it can take some trial and error to find the right teacher. This is true especially if you are looking through an online teacher directory that doesn't do a great job of screening their teachers. You can waste hours scrolling through teacher profiles (which all seem to have five star ratings), only to be disappointed with the one you chose.

- Teachers aren't free. But getting a private teacher is a lot more affordable than you think...

Sure, there are plenty of "high end" teachers who will try to charge you as much as US$60-80/hour. On the "low end," you can probably find someone for less than US$10/hour, although they are usually unqualified tutors who can barely explain things better than your average native speaker.

Verbalicity has a good offer of "high-end" teaching for as little as US$15/hour. You can try out the first lesson for free. Go to: https://verbalicity.com

Of course, there are plenty of people who have learned Dutch without a teacher. Doing a language exchange or going to a meetup is certainly better than not speaking at all, but it will take much longer to learn, and you may be tempted to give up in the process.

So, if you've got a busy schedule and want to learn Dutch fast, then getting a teacher is definitely the best way to go.

Road Map: Zero to Conversational

We've just isolated some of the key concepts and methods that make up the best ways to learn Dutch. Now let's go through the three stages of learning. For each stage, we'll recap what the main goals and recommended method of learning are and offer some more tips on how to progress as quickly as possible.

Stage 1: Introduction

This stage is for absolute beginners. If you already have some knowledge of Dutch or are used to hearing it, then you can skip to the next stage.

Objective:

The idea is to get a brief introduction to Dutch with the goal of familiarizing yourself with the following:

- What spoken Dutch sounds like.
- How it feels to pronounce Dutch words.
- A few basic phrases.

This helps you acclimatize to learning a new language and gets you used to listening and speaking right away.

After this stage, you probably will have some basic phrases under your belt, like "My name is…", "Where are you from?" and "What time is it?"

How to do it:

Start with a free audio course or one of the popular apps. Ideally, it should be a guided course that's easy to follow. Here are some examples:

- One Minute Dutch audio course and, Survival Dutch

- The first few episodes of " NOS Jeugdjournaal" just run a search on Google and you can pick your preference
- Get Memrise (https://www.memrise.com) and start using their basic Dutch course, or use other free apps like Duolingo (https://www.duolingo.com).

"Wait," you are no doubt be saying to yourself, "didn't he say that apps can't teach you a language?"

That's true. But I didn't say they couldn't help, and at this point in time, all you're trying to do is get your bearings and get comfortable with listening and repeating.

You probably only need about 30 minutes a day, and this introductory stage should last no more than a few weeks.

Afterward, you can cut down or stop using these resources altogether because, although they are fine as an introduction, they are slow and inefficient. You should move on to better options, which we'll cover next.

Tip for this stage:

Focus on pronunciation

Try to get your pronunciation right from the very beginning. When you hear the Dutch recording, make sure you repeat it out loud.

At first, repeat each word slowly, syllable by syllable, until you can mimic the sounds almost perfectly. If necessary, record yourself speaking and listen back.

Once you're satisfied that you're saying it right, then repeat it over and over again until it feels natural.

Stage 2: Beginner

Objective:

At this stage, the goal is to build a solid foundation for yourself in terms of basic grammar and vocabulary, put your thoughts into complete sentences, and be confident enough to talk to people.

At the end of this stage, you want to be able to have basic conversations that involve exchanging information, asking for things, and talking about work, family, and your interests.

Effectively, you want to be at an upper-beginner level.

How to do it:
For the beginner stage, the best way to learn Dutch is to choose one of these two options:

Option 1:
- Textbook
- Speaking practice: friends, meetups, exchanges, Skype.
- Flashcards (optional)

Using a textbook might seem old-fashioned, but it is still probably the best way for a beginner to learn the grammatical rules of Dutch. The reason why a textbook is effective is that it teaches you in a structured way. It takes you through a progression that slowly builds on each concept, step by step.

For each chapter of the textbook that you go through, study the dialogues and make sure you do all the practice exercises. Ideally, you should try to find additional exercises online related to the concept you just learned.

Just like most forms of learning, a textbook can't actually teach you to speak. So, for each concept you learn, you need to be practicing it with real people.

You can use a combination of friends, meetups, or language exchanges to get your practice in. At this point, you are not having full conversations yet (nor should you try to). Try practicing phrases and some short dialogues or scenarios. But nevertheless, you should aim for one to two hours per week of speaking practice.

Option 2:

- Learn with a Dutch teacher in person or online
- Flashcards (optional)

When you learn with a teacher, you get step-by-step guidance and speaking practice all in one package.

A good Dutch teacher will send or give you textbook materials and all the practice exercises you'll ever need, so there is no need to look for materials on your own. You even get homework, just like in school.

A teacher can also explain grammar to you in different ways and answer your questions if you don't understand. This is a big advantage over someone who is just studying on their own.

Being able to practice what you learned immediately through speaking is another advantage. For example, you might spend the first half of a lesson going over the conjugations of the Imperfect tense and then spend the second half the lesson practicing it verbally through question and answer, storytelling, and other fun exercises.

Flashcards

It is never too early to start using flashcards to help you remember words.

But especially if you've chosen Option 1, it might be a little overwhelming to be studying while trying to find practice opportunities, and you don't want to add another method like flashcards to distract you from that.

Remember the 80/20 rule. It is better to focus on a few things that have the highest impact.

But if you feel like you're having trouble remembering new words or grammar conjugations, then it's probably time to incorporate flashcards into your routine.

Tips for this stage:

Don't jump ahead
It might be tempting to immediately work your way through a textbook from cover to cover, but this will just overload you with information.

A lot of people make the mistake of diving too deep into the grammar without making sure that they fully understand and have practiced each concept before moving on to the next. If in doubt, spend more time reviewing what you've already learned.

Be strategic about your vocabulary
Focus on memorizing the most useful words that will make it easier for you to practice speaking. Highly useful words include "power verbs" and "connectors." You can find these online or in any decent text book

If you master these types of words, your speech will come out more naturally, and it will make you sound more fluent than you actually are at this point. This can give you a much-needed boost of confidence because, at this stage, it can still be scary to be out there talking to people.

Intermediate
Objective:

This stage is all about expanding your horizons. It's about greatly increasing your vocabulary, comprehension skills, and confidence in using Dutch in a variety of situations.

At the end of this stage, you want to be able to express yourself freely and talk about different topics, like what's happening in the news, your hopes and dreams, or your opinion on a particular subject.

You're still going to make plenty of mistakes, and your grammar won't be perfect, but the goal is to be able to get your ideas across, whatever they may be. If you can do that, you'll reach the upper intermediate level and be considered **conversationally fluent.**

Some may choose to improve their Dutch even further, to more advanced levels, but for many people, this is this level where you can fully enjoy the rewards of being able to speak Dutch.

How to do it:

Based on the two options from the beginner stage, we can make a few adjustments for the intermediate level:

Option 1:

- Speaking practice (*friends, meetups, exchanges*)
- Reading and listening
- Flashcards
- Textbooks (*optional*)

Option 2:

- Learn with a Dutch teacher

- Reading and listening
- Flashcards

Speaking practice

To move into the intermediate stage, speaking becomes even more important. By now you should be ramping up your speaking practice to a **minimum of two to three hours per week**.

Whereas you were previously practicing short phrases or dialogues, you should now be able to have more full-fledged conversations because you know more vocabulary and grammar.

If you are learning with a teacher, you should know them pretty well by now, so you can have deeper conversations about more diverse topics. Your teacher can also start to speak a little bit faster to help train your ear.

Active Reading/Listening

This is the stage where active reading and listening start to shine. You know enough Dutch now that you can really take advantage of movies, TV, radio, podcasts, books, and articles.

You won't understand 100% of what you read and hear. Heck, maybe you only understand 50-60% at this point, but that is enough to get the gist of what is going on. If you're watching TV shows or movies, turn on Dutch subtitles (Netflix is great for this). Reading and listening at the same time will get you the best results.

Try to find material that is interesting to you. This way, you can enjoy the process of listening and reading, which can become a source of motivation. You'll also pick up Dutch that is relevant and useful to you personally.

Remember, "Active" means giving it your full attention. Try your best to understand it and pay attention to the grammar and vocabulary and the context in which they are being used. If there is anything you don't understand, write it down so you can look it up later, or ask your teacher during your next lesson.

Flashcards

A big part of going from beginner to intermediate is significantly increasing your vocabulary. By now, you will have already learned all the "easy" words, and to further build your vocabulary, you need to be very deliberate about remembering all the new words you are exposed to every day.

Using flashcard apps like Anki or Memrise can really help commit them to memory. You can practice in five-minute chunks (while waiting for the bus, etc.) for a total of 10-20 minutes a day to get great results.

Textbook

A textbook is not mandatory at this point. You've learned most of the important grammar, and now the focus should be to practice it until you can use it fluidly.

Of course, there are always more advanced grammar concepts to learn, but they tend to be used very sparingly in everyday conversations.

Tips for this stage:
Learning formula

Your "routine" for learning new material should look something like this:

- You're exposed to new Dutch vocabulary and grammar through your teacher and textbook or by listening and reading.
- Review it using flashcards.
- Speak it until it becomes second nature.

For example, you hear a phrase on a Dutch TV show which you are not familiar with.

You look up the meaning and then create a new flashcard in Anki.
The next day, the flashcard pops up, and you review it.

A few days later, you head to your Dutch meetup, and during a conversation bring up the phrase

Staying Motivated
When you reach the intermediate stage, you may feel like you're not progressing as fast as you did before. In fact, there will be times where you feel like you aren't improving at all.

This is the classic "dip" that comes with learning any skill, and Dutch is no exception.

This happens because you've already learned a lot of the "low-hanging fruit." What you are learning now is more incremental and takes longer for everything to click in your mind.

To overcome the dip, you need to trust the process and be disciplined when it comes to the learning formula.

Your teacher can really help you stay motivated by creating a plan that guides you to new things you should learn and older concepts you should be reviewing, as well as giving you feedback on what you are doing well and what you need to improve on.

Time Frame

So, how long does it take to learn Dutch using this road map?

I'm not going to lie to you and say that you can become fluent in 30 days. Maybe some people can, but most of us lead busy lives, with jobs, families, and other responsibilities competing for our time.

If you are learning with a Dutch teacher (Option 2), I believe that you can go from zero to conversationally fluent in **8–12 months** using the methods in this road map.

This assumes that you can spend **one hour per day** working on your Dutch, whether that's the actual Dutch lessons themselves, reviewing flashcards, or actively listening and reading.

This timeframe is just an estimate because, obviously, everyone learns at a different pace. Of course, the more time you dedicate to learning Dutch, the faster you'll progress.

If you decide to go at it alone (Option 1), it will take a lot longer. But if you follow the best way to learn Dutch as outlined in the road map, stay disciplined, and make sure you consistently get enough conversation practice, you'll get there eventually.

Final Thoughts

Absolutely anyone can learn Dutch.

It doesn't matter whether or not you have a talent for languages or whether you are a naturally fast learner.

At the end of the day, learning Dutch is about motivation, focus, and time.

If you've got all three of these things and you commit to speaking rather than just learning the "stuff" of Dutch, then you simply cannot fail.

And of course, don't forget to have FUN! The process should be as enjoyable as the end goal.

CHAPTER FIFTEEN

LEARNING WITHOUT TRYING

Remember the story about the lazy bricklayer way back in Chapter One? Well, to recap, the lazy way, or the way that involves the least amount of work, is most often the smartest way to do things.

Do the things that involve the least amount of work when learning a language. Engage in effortless language learning, not completely effortless, of course, but as effortless as possible.

The word "effortless" in this context is borrowed from two sources. One is AJ Hoge, who is a great teacher of English. His channel and website are both called Effortless English. The other source is Taoist philosophy.

Effortlessness and the Parable of the Crooked Tree

When the linguist Steve Kaufmann (who, incidentally, can speak over 20 languages) wrote his book *The Linguist: A Personal Guide to Language Learning*, he began with what he called "The Parable of the Crooked Tree."

The author of the parable was Zhuangzi, an early exponent of Taoism, a school of Chinese philosophy from over two thousand years ago. Zhuangzi's basic principle in life was to follow what was natural, what was effortless, and not try to force things.

Typically, the Taoist philosophy was in opposition to Confucianism, which prescribed rules of what you should and shouldn't do to be a great person. Confucianism is full of admonishments on how you should behave. As is often the case with prescriptive philosophies or religions, these "commandments" attempt to set the boundaries of correct behavior. Zhuangzi was different. He advised people to follow their own natures and to not resist the world around them. This effortless non-resistance would help them learn better and be happier.

In Zhuangzi's parable of the crooked tree, his friend Huizi tells him that a tree they are both observing is crooked because the lumber is not good for anything, like Zhuangzi's philosophy.

"Neither your philosophy nor the tree is good for anything," says Huizi.

Zhuangzi replies, "You say that because you don't know how to use them. You have to use things for the purpose intended and understand their true nature. You can sit underneath a crooked tree and enjoy its shade, for example. If you understand the true nature of things, you will be able to use them to achieve your goals."

I'm in the lumber business, and sometimes those gnarly old trees produce very expensive and decorative wood.

Compared to trees in a planted forest, their wood is less uniform and less suitable for industrial end uses. We just have to accept these more individualistic trees as they are and appreciate what they bring. Zhuangzi defends his philosophy, saying it is useful if we accept its nature and know how to use it.

Zhuangi's philosophy was based on effortlessness, "wu wei" (无为) in Chinese. In other words, if you want to learn better, stop resisting; go with the flow. That has always been my approach. Language learning does require some effort, of course, but we learn best when effort is minimized and pleasure is maximized.

Let's look at something that requires effort but is also usually enjoyable: reading.

If you are reading in a language that you read well and you come across a few unknown words, you usually don't look up those unknown words in a dictionary because it's too much trouble and you have usually worked out the meaning because of the context.

So, what happens if you are reading something in Dutch as a beginner and have to constantly resort to dictionaries? They are no longer the learning aid they once were but become a chore and a block to enjoying reading in the way you are accustomed. And what's worse, if you don't memorize these new words' meanings, you will keep on getting bogged down. So, is there a better or easier way to start off reading in Dutch - an effortless way?

Thankfully, yes, there is. It is called LingQ (https://www.lingq.com/en). You can read in Dutch using LingQ on your computer, laptop, iPad, or smartphone.

When you look up a word in LingQ, it's highlighted. The word then appears highlighted in any subsequent material so you are reminded that you've looked it up before. You can see the meaning straight away, and eventually it becomes part of you, without any effort.

You are not just looking words up in a dictionary and then forgetting them. You are creating your own personal database of words and phrases for easy review as you continue reading.

Steve Kaufmann highly recommends this as a way of learning a language, and he should know. He has similar practical thoughts on grammar:

When I read grammar – and I believe we should occasionally read grammar rules as it helps give us a sense of the language – I don't try to remember anything.
I don't try to learn or understand anything. I just treat it as a spark, an exposure of something that might help me eventually get a sense of the language. I don't worry about grammar. I know it will gradually become clearer for me.

Have you ever noticed how some people can learn languages effortlessly (Steve Kaufmann would be one), getting to fluency faster with pen and paper than others do with a bag full of textbooks and phone-full of learning apps?

Everything about their learning seems effortless, and every new word and expression they learn is used with utmost confidence.

What is it about these individuals that sets them apart?

Every language learner strives for this effortlessly cool way of learning, where study ceases to be a chore and language usage becomes commonplace.

While it may seem like these individuals were born with a natural linguistic talent, it actually all comes down to a few simple habits these super-learners integrate into their daily life.

Here's a short list, along with some tips on implementing these habits in your daily life and becoming the confident speaker you want to be.
Note: You do not have to follow these recommendations exactly; adapt them to your lifestyle and unique personality.

Review before learning, even if it means you don't have time or energy to learn more.

Effective language learners know that what you don't review, you forget forever, and forgetting means that all that time you've spent learning the new word or expression has been put to waste.

That is why you should always prioritize reviewing above learning and start every study session by going over your past notes and flashcards.

That way, if you realize halfway through that you're just too exhausted to make the progress you hoped for, you've at least made sure you don't regress by activating all the connections already in your brain!

Tip: Never learn something new before you review what you know already.

Study a little bit every day and don't mistake the illusion of progress for actual improvement.

Effective language learners understand that binge-learning is but an illusion of progress.

When you try to learn long lists of vocabulary all at once or leaf through a textbook, chapter after chapter, without giving the necessary thought to the information within, your brain starts a tally that addictively goes up with every leaf.

The problem is, that mental counter represents the number of words and lessons you've seen, not the information you can actually use, or even remember the next morning.

Binge learning is extremely motivating at the beginning, but it consistently leads to burnout when the rational part of your brain finally realizes that all this euphoria was, in fact, unjustified.

Tip: Study in small chunks every day, even if for just five or 10 minutes.

Have a clear goal and use the language for something you already enjoy.

Effective learners realize that you can't learn a language without motivation that comes from the prospect of using it in the context you're passionate about.

For example: If you love horses, include equestrian themes throughout your learning. If you enjoy scuba diving like me, include Dutch-speaking scuba-diving sites in your learning.

Tip: Use the language in the context of the topics you're passionate about and the activities you enjoy.

Avoid having a closet full of unopened textbooks or a phone full of learning apps.

Effective language learners know that there's no silver bullet to language learning, so they don't waste time searching for it. They choose an effective method quickly and stick to it until there is a real need to change.

One mistake beginners in language learning fall victim to again and again is going on a shopping spree for learning resources only to realize that they are spending more time scavenging for new ways to learn than actually learning.

It's good to choose a methodology that works for you, but it's even more important to do so quickly and get back to learning.

Tip: Spend a week researching different learning methods, select one or two that suit you best, and stick with them until you've read them cover to cover or identify a clear need to supplement them with another resource.

Strike a balance between consuming the language and using it to convey your thoughts.

Effective learners value output as much as input and make sure to write or say a new word out loud every time they read or listen to one.

There are countless examples of language learners who spend all their time cramming vocabulary only to find themselves at a loss for words when thrown into a real-life conversation.

There are also countless examples of those who dedicate every minute to speaking to friends and blogging in the target language. Such students are often remarkably fluent in their specific topic of interest or when they speak to their usual interlocutors, but they can struggle to produce a single coherent sentence outside of that context.

No matter your ultimate goal, it is crucial to learn languages in a balanced way. Reading and listening to native material on a diverse range of topics will enrich your own expressiveness. Using new words and expressions you've picked up from others will cement them in your memory.

Tip: Dedicate as much time to speaking and writing as to reading and listening and try to regularly wander into topics outside your comfort zone.

You will often fail, so celebrate your mistakes as opportunities to get better.

Effective learners value mistakes and misunderstandings as opportunities to learn and improve.

Everyone remembers Henry Ford's Model T, but what preceded it was a very imperfect Model A. Ford's mechanics gathered real-world insight into all its deficiencies and fixed them one at a time before coming up with the icon of the automotive history.

The only way to improve is to start using new expressions right after you learn them, make mistakes, and use those mistakes to improve your abilities.

It's not a failure to use the wrong grammar or make a blatant spelling mistake. The only true failure is when you don't learn from the mess-up or use it as an excuse to give up.

Tip: Don't look at mistakes as failures but rather as immediate opportunities to improve your language abilities.

Always be attentive and try to imitate the way native speakers use the language.

Effective learners mimic what expressions native speakers use in a given context, how they pronounce them, and what gestures they choose to reinforce their message.

Textbooks and dictionaries are great at teaching you what's grammatically correct, but they can't guide you to speak naturally in day-to-day situations. An expression that would give you full marks on a test, and pass every spell check, may sound absolutely jarring in the real world.

The best way to learn the language as it is actually spoken is to put yourself in context with native speakers and listen carefully to what they say! Then note down the natural sentence patterns you hear and use them yourself.

Next time you're queuing up for a matcha latte, stop trying to imagine the conversation you'll have with the barista and instead listen to the conversations she's having with other clients!

Tip: Always be attentive to what native speakers say in any given situation and note down the sentence patterns they use.

Let's leave this chapter by just recapping some of the major points made throughout this book:

- Something inside you has got to want to learn the language.
- Ignore grammar at the beginning and concentrate instead on learning new words.
- Work on learning the most commonly used words and forget about words that are rarely ever used.
- Make language learning automatic by listening, reading, and digesting the language wherever you can.
- And finally, find ways to make learning fun by reading new books, subscribing to blogs, translating street signs, listening to music, or conversing with strangers.

I leave you with the immortal words of Fatboy Slim: *"Just lay back and let the big beat lead you."*

CONCLUSION

If you have learned one thing from this book, I hope it is that the most effective learning is not obtained by trying too hard. If you fill your head with useless vocabulary and grammar rules you do not need to speak Dutch, eventually you will burn out and give up. Just keep to the bare minimum when starting out, find what works for you, and stick with that until something more effective comes your way.

You will have gathered by now that learning to speak Dutch is different from just learning Dutch. The emphasis is always on speaking. and understanding.

Learn at your own pace; do not force it. Find your own way. It is better to go slowly but surely rather than rush. The tortoise will always do better than the hare in language learning.

My abiding hope is that by the end of this book, you will have found your own path to speaking Dutch fluently and effortlessly.

Vaarwel!

BIBLIOGRAPHY / ONLINE RESOURCES

I have literally begged, borrowed, or stolen a lot of the content of this book, and I am indebted to the authors, teachers, website owners, app writers, and bloggers who have spent valuable time putting resources online or in print to help people learn a new language. I will list them after this brief epilogue.

I urge you to use the resources they have made available. Find what works for you. It may be a combination of all or some of them, or even just one. If you can't afford to buy their stuff, use the free stuff until you can. It will be well worth it.

By the way, I do not receive any sort of commission or kickback for recommending any of the courses, websites, blogs, or apps mentioned below. The fact that I have included them in this book is based purely on merit. Any of these *helpers* will stand you in good stead.

I was lucky. I started learning new languages when I was young, sometimes out of necessity (just to be understood by my peers) and sometimes out of precocious curiosity. I was also - and still am - filled with wanderlust and spent my mid- and late-teenage years hitchhiking around Europe (without a penny to my name and devoid of any dictionary, travel guide, or even map). "Ah," I hear you say, "that's why it was so easy for you, but I'm an adult, and I have a million things on my mind and a trillion things to do. It's so easy when you are a kid. You don't have to worry about anything else apart from living. I have so many responsibilities."

Yes and no. Kids do worry about a spectacular amount of things, and a lot of their time is tied up with doing things they also consider important. What makes the difference with learning like a child is that children learn or assimilate a language faster because, one, they have fewer hang-ups about making mistakes and interacting with other language speakers, and two, they learn better when they are having fun and are interested. This is when they are seemingly picking up the language effortlessly.

My aim is to rekindle some of that emotion in you. Stick your thumb in the air, hitch a lift from whatever resource gets you moving, sit back, and enjoy the ride. Make this journey fun and exciting, and you will speak Dutch at the end of it.

- Anki (https://apps.ankiweb.net/) SRS (spaced repetition software) with intelligent flashcards.
- De Telegraaf (https://www.telegraaf.nl/) Online Dutch newspaper.
- CoffeeBreak Dutch (https://radiolingua.com/) Learn Dutch on your coffee break.
- ConversationExchange (https://www.conversationexchange.com) Practice with native speakers in your area.
- Duolingo (https://www.duolingo.com/) Fun podcast for learning Dutch.

- FluentU (https://www.fluentu.com/en/) SRS app and language immersion online.
- Dutchpod 101 (https://www.dutchpod101.com/) podcast for real beginners.
- italki (https://www.italki.com/) Online teaching and conversation resource.
- Languages-Direct (https://www.languages-direct.com/) Dutch printed and audio materials audio magazine.
- LingQ (https://www.lingq.com/en/) Online reading resource.
- Meetup (https://www.meetup.com/) Online language exchange.
- Memrise (https://www.memrise.com/) Memory techniques to speed up language learning.
- My Language Exchange (mylanguageexchange.com) Online language exchange community.
- stephenhernandez.co.uk (https://stephenhernandez.co.uk/) Free tips on how to improve your language learning.
- SuperMemo (https://www.supermemo.com/en) SRS app.
- The Intrepid Guide Survival Dutch travel phrase guide with pronunciation.
- The Positivity Blog (https://www.positivityblog.com/) Henrik Edberg's positivity blog.
- Verbalicity (https://verbalicity.com/) One-on-one online lessons with native teachers.

Printed in Great Britain
by Amazon